Okinawa

Books by Robert Leckie

Okinawa

THE LAST BATTLE OF

WORLD WAR II

ROBERT LECKIE

VIKING

VIKING
Published by the Penguin Group
Penguin Books USA Inc., 375 Hudson Street,
New York, New York 10014, U.S.A.
Penguin Books Ltd, 27 Wrights Lane, London W8 5TZ, England
Penguin Books Australia Ltd, Ringwood, Victoria, Australia
Penguin Books Canada Ltd, 10 Alcorn Avenue,
Toronto, Ontario, Canada M4V 3B2
Penguin Books (N.Z.) Ltd, 182–190 Wairau Road,
Auckland 10, New Zealand

Penguin Books Ltd, Registered Offices:
Harmondsworth, Middlesex, England

First published in 1995 by Viking Penguin,
a division of Penguin Books USA Inc.

10 9 8 7 6 5 4 3 2 1

LIBRARY OF CONGRESS CATALOGING-IN-PUBLICATION DATA
Leckie, Robert.
Okinawa: the last battle of World War II / Robert Leckie
p.   cm.
Includes index.
ISBN 0-670-84716-X
1. World War, 1939–1945—Campaigns—Japan—Okinawa Island.
2. Okinawa Island (Japan)—History.   I. Title.
D767.99.O45L43   1995
940.54'25—dc20   94-39145

This book is printed on acid-free paper.
∞

Printed in the United States of America
Set in Janson Text
Designed by Francesca Belanger

To My Fourth Grandson,
Sean Michael Leckie

Contents

x   Contents

Okinawa

Why Okinawa?

CHAPTER ONE

On September 29, 1944, Fleet Admiral Chester Nimitz, commander of the Pacific Ocean Area (POA), and Fleet Admiral Ernest King, chief of U.S. Naval Operations, conferred in San Francisco on the next steps to be taken to deliver the final crusher to a staggering Japan. This was the conference's stated purpose, but the unspoken objective was to persuade the irascible, often-inflexible King to accept Nimitz's battle plan, instead of King's own.

This would not be easy, for the tall, lean, hard, humorless King was known to be "so tough he shaves with a blowtorch." Indeed, his civilian chief, Secretary of the Navy Frank Knox, had ordered from Tiffany's a silver miniature blowtorch with that inscription on it. Thus, there was some trepidation among Nimitz and his Army chiefs—Lieutenant General Simon Bolivar Buckner of Army Ground Forces (POA) and Lieutenant General Millard Harmon of the newly formed Army Air Forces (POA)—as well as Admiral Raymond Spruance, alternate chief with Fleet Admiral William "Bull" Halsey, of Nimitz's battle fleet.* They knew that

---

* When Spruance commanded this enormous concentration of naval striking power, it was called "Task Force Fifty-eight"; when Bull Halsey's flag was flown it was "Task Force Thirty-eight."

1

King was convinced the next operation in the Pacific should be landings on the big island of Formosa off the Chinese southeastern coast. If Nimitz and staff could persuade King to accept General of the Armies Douglas MacArthur's plan to invade Luzon in the Philippines rather than Formosa, the conference would end in a rare and high note of interservice cooperation.

Each of the conferees was assigned a luxurious suite in the elegant Saint Francis Hotel, assembling in Admiral King's opulent quarters for three days of discussions. Here they were served epicurean meals that were not often to be found on the menu in the Saint Francis dining rooms (wartime rationing then being in effect). Here also—and sometimes in the plainer Sea Frontier headquarters, where maps and logistic tables were more readily available—Nimitz presented his chief with one of those carefully drawn memoranda for which he was justly celebrated. With an outward calm and precision that did not reflect his inner apprehension, the pink-cheeked, white-haired, baby-faced Nimitz was careful not to provoke the stern-faced, short-fused Admiral "Adamant" while he explained exactly why King's cherished invasion of Formosa would be impossible to mount at that time.

First, defending that huge island now known as Taiwan, the Japanese had a full field army much too strong to be attacked by American forces then available in the Pacific, a point vigorously supported by both Buckner and Harmon.

Second, the casualty estimate, based upon U.S. losses of 17,000 dead and wounded while eliminating 32,000 dug-in Japanese on the island of Saipan, would reach at least 150,000 or more, a slaughter that POA's resources could not bear and the American public would never supinely accept. Conversely, MacArthur—always ready and happy to predict minimal losses in any of his own operations—had estimated Luzon could be taken with comparatively moderate casualties.

Throughout this recital Ernest King's face remained stony. It is possible—though not reported anywhere—that at the introduction of the name of Douglas MacArthur, one of the admiral's eyelids might have flickered. But Nimitz was prepared for this moment, for he had long ago learned that you cannot take without giving, and Nimitz would give with an alternative to King's cherished plan. He suggested to his chief that if he acquiesced in MacArthur's liberation of Luzon and recapture of Manila, these victories would clear the Pacific for the direct invasion of Japan's home islands by seizing Iwo Jima and Okinawa and using them as staging areas. King's eyebrows rose as Nimitz continued: this would completely sever Japan from her oil sources in Borneo, Sumatra, and Burma, and without this lifeblood of war her fleets could not sail, her airplanes fly, her vehicles roll, or her industries produce. Equally satisfying, from Okinawa and Iwo the giant B-29s or Superforts could intensify their bombardment of Japan proper and might conceivably even bomb Nippon into submission without the necessity of invading her home islands.

Admiral King listened intently to Nimitz's recital, shooting out tough, incisive questions. He admitted that he had read a Joint Chiefs' report questioning the feasibility of a Formosa invasion, although he did wonder openly about the wisdom of hitting Iwo only 760 miles from Japan and within the Prefecture of Tokyo itself. Turning to Admiral Spruance, who three months earlier had informed the Navy chief that he favored attacking Okinawa, he asked: "Haven't you something to say? I thought that Okinawa was your baby." Never a man to allow himself to be caught between the upper and nether millstones of command, Spruance replied that he thought his direct superior—Nimitz— had summarized the situation nicely, and he had nothing to add.

To the Nimitz team's gratified surprise, Admiral Adamant graciously agreed to substitute Iwo and Okinawa for his cherished Formosa plan, even though that meant he must put his eagerness to help China on hold. It might have been that Nimitz's proposal was attractive to him because it delayed the politically explosive question of who would be the Supreme Allied Commander in the

Pacific: Nimitz or MacArthur? For years Douglas MacArthur had actively sought that eminence, almost insanely jealous as he was of the title Supreme Allied Commander, European Theater, held by his "former clerk," Dwight Eisenhower. To that end he had cultivated the support of powerful politicians and the conservative stateside press, desisting only when an exasperated Franklin Delano Roosevelt informed him that if the Pacific were to have a Supreme Commander, it would be Nimitz. This way, King may have reasoned, his decision—bound to be popular with neither side in the abrasive Army-Navy rivalry of World War II—could be delayed until the actual invasion of Japan, if there were such an operation, for both Nimitz and King dreaded the fearful carnage, both American and Japanese, that might occur if it were attempted. As sailors they understood perhaps better than the always-optimistic soldier MacArthur the terrible consequences if such a gigantic amphibious operation were to fail.

So the conference in San Francisco ended on a happy note, with King returning to Washington to report his approval to his comrades on the Joint Chiefs, and Nimitz with his flag officers going back to Hawaii to plan for the new operations and especially for Iwo and *Iceberg*, the code name for Okinawa.

Okinawa lies at the midpoint of the Ryukyu Islands* and almost between Formosa (Taiwan), 500 nautical miles to the southwest, and Kyushu, 375 miles to the north.

In ancient times Okinawa was a dependency of China, paying an annual tribute to the Imperial Court at Peking. The group of islands was called *Liu-chi'u*, the Chinese word usually pronounced "Loo Choo," meaning either "pendant ball" or "bubbles floating

---

* Because there is no hard-and-fast rule for translating Japanese geographical terms—*shoto*, meaning various islands or group of islands; *gunto* or *retto*, a group of islands; *shima* or *jima*, an island; or *ie*, an islet—this narrative will use the general English words for the same.

on water"; but after annexation by Japan in 1879, their new lords, who have great difficulty pronouncing the "L" sound, changed their name to Ryukyu.

These islands lie southwest of Japan proper, northeast of Formosa and the Philippines, and west of the Bonins, which include Iwo Jima. Peaks of drowned mountains, they stretch in an arc about 790 miles long between Kyushu and Formosa. Approximately in the center of the arc is the Okinawa Group of some fifty islands clustering around the largest of them, Okinawa: 60 miles long (running generally north to south), from 2 to 18 miles wide, and covering 485 square miles. Obviously such a base so close to Japan, able to support dozens of airfields, as well as dozens of divisions together with all manner of warships anchored either in the enormous Hagushi Anchorage off the west coast or the equally valuable Nakagusuku Bay off the southeast shore, would be almost "another England"—the staging area for the Allied invasion of Europe—for the waterborne attack upon Japan.

In 1945 Okinawa had a population of about five hundred thousand, of whom roughly 60 percent lived in the southern third, much more amenable than the rugged and mountainous north above the two-mile-wide Isthmus of Ishikawa.

Originally, Okinawans resembled Japanese, but an influx of Malay, Chinese, Mongol, and other races left them smaller and fuller of face than their new masters from the north. They were also among the most docile people in the world. They had no history of war, neither making nor carrying arms. (When a traveler informed Napoléon of this fact, the Corsican conqueror was indignant.) Although Jesus, Allah, and Confucius had been to Okinawa, their missionaries persuaded few if any natives to renounce their primitive animist religion based on a mystical reverence for fire and hearth and worship of the bones of their ancestors. These were placed in urns kept inside fairly large lyre-shaped tombs, which the Japanese, with their customary indifference to the feelings of any race but their own, began to fortify

with machine guns and cannon at the outbreak of the war. Okinawan standards of living were low, and the Japanese made no
attempt to raise them.

Generally the haughty Nipponese despised the Okinawans as
inferior people and were content to regard them as hewers of
wood and drawers of water, useful with their small-scale farms to
supply them—and eventually their troops—with sugarcane, sweet
potatoes, rice, and soybeans. Aside from teachers trained in Japan,
almost all Okinawans—like the Amerindians of America—had no
desire to enjoy the blessings of industrial society, but were content
to live as their ancestors had lived in tiny villages of about one
hundred people or towns numbering one thousand. Although the
Japanese, for all of their contempt for them, had drafted many
young Okinawan males into their militia, on the whole Japanese
troops in the Great Loo Choo were hated with a quiet and sullen
resentment similar to the attitude of the early American colonists
toward the British redcoats quartered in their homes. Although
the Japanese and Okinawan languages are alike, neither is intel-
ligible to the other race.

The southern third of the island below Ishikawa, where most
of the fighting would rage, is rolling, hilly country lower than the
mountainous, jumbled North, but actually much easier to defend.
Steep, natural escarpments, ravines, and terraces—as well as
ridges abounding in natural caves—were generally aligned east
and west across the island. This meant that an attacking force
must engage in the most difficult warfare: "cross-hatch" fighting.
There were no north-south ridges with river valleys or passes
through which troops might move easily. Thus, moving south,
the Americans would encounter a succession of these heavily fortified east-west ridges, and each time one fell, a new one would
have to be assaulted.

The only two-way decent road in the South was in the Naha-
Shuri area: Naha, the new port and commercial center; Shuri, the
capital of the ancient Okinawa kings. Even these were impassable

during the torrential rains that regularly turned the entire island, except for the limestone ridges, into a sea of mud—for the skies of the Great Loo Choo were capable of pouring out eleven inches of rainfall in a single day.

Just as inimical to health or endurance was an enervating humidity unrivaled even by Eritrea or the Belgian Congo, and the best description of the country lanes over which a modern, mechanized army would have to travel is an American soldier's wry comment: "Okinawa had an excellent network of bad roads."

Shuri Castle was the point of Okinawa's defensive arrowhead. It lay on high ground overlooking Naha to the east (or right, as it would face the American invaders). Beneath it an ancient cave system was being extended and strengthened to provide a completely safe bomb- and shell-proof headquarters for the Japanese Thirty-second Army. Heavy guns emplaced nearby could bombard any part of southern Okinawa. If the Americans, in spite of heavy losses, were able to penetrate Shuri's outer defenses, the defending Japanese could withdraw toward the center. So long as Shuri remained unconquered, so did Okinawa.

These fortifications resembled the blood-soaked caves and fissures of Peleliu, a drowned coral mountain that had heaved itself above the sea. But Okinawa's were man-made; its soft coral and limestone could be grubbed up with pick and shovel, and small natural caves expanded to hold as many men as a company of two hundred or more. The fill thus removed was eminently useful in building barricades that, when soaked with water and baked by the sun, were almost as hard as concrete. But Peleliu was only six miles long by two miles wide, while southern Okinawa was about twenty miles long and in some places eighteen miles wide.

This, then, was the terrible fortified terrain that would confront the Americans when they came storming ashore in the spring of 1945. Even worse—for the seamen of the U.S. Navy, at least—would be the Japanese new weapon of the *kamikaze*.

Japan at Bay

CHAPTER TWO

No one—and especially not the members of Japanese Imperial General Headquarters or the United States Joint Chiefs of Staff—expected Okinawa to be the last battle of World War II. Why the surprise? The Joint Chiefs, having woefully underestimated enemy striking power at the beginning of the Pacific War, had just as grievously exaggerated it at the end.

Actually, as some perceptive Okinawans were already privately assuring each other: "*Nippon ga maketa.* Japan is finished." In early 1945, after the conquest of Iwo Jima by three Marine divisions, the island nation so vulnerable to aerial and submarine warfare had been almost completely severed from its stolen Pacific empire in "the land of eternal summer." Leyte in the Philippines had been assaulted the previous October by an American amphibious force under General of the Armies Douglas MacArthur, and in the same month the U.S. Navy had destroyed the remnants of the once-proud Japanese Navy in the Battle of Leyte Gulf. On January 9, Luzon in the Philippines was invaded, and on February 16–17, like a "typhoon of steel," the fast carriers of the U.S. Navy launched the first naval air raids on Tokyo Bay. A week later

Manila was overrun by those American "devils in baggy pants."
In late March Iwo fell to three Marine divisions in the bloodiest
battle in the annals of American arms. Not only was Old Glory
enshrined forever in American military history by the historic
flag-raising atop Mount Suribachi, but more important strategi-
cally and more dreadful for Japanese fears was the capture of
this insignificant little speck of black volcanic ash—a cinder clog,
4½ miles long and 2½ miles wide—for it guaranteed that the
devastating raids on Japan by the new giant B-29 U.S. Army Air
Force bombers would continue and even rise in fury.

Iwo became a base from which the Superforts could fly closer
to the Japanese capital undetected and under protection of Iwo-
based American fighter planes. Perhaps even more welcome to
these gallant airmen, crippled B-29s unable to make the fifteen-
hundred-mile flight back to Saipan could now touch down safely
on tiny Iwo; or if shot down off the shores of Nippon, could even
be reached by Iwo-based Dumbo rescue planes. Thus, not only
could these exorbitantly expensive aerial elephants be saved, but
their truly more valuable crews as well. On the night of March 9,
to prove their worth and sound the requiem of the "unconquer-
able" island empire, the Superforts already striking Tokyo, Na-
goya, Osaka, and Kobe in pulverizing three-hundred-plane raids
came down to six thousand feet over Tokyo to loose the dreadful
firebombs that consumed a quarter of a million houses and made
a million human beings homeless while killing 83,800 people in
the most lethal air raid in history—even exceeding the death and
destruction of the atomic-bomb strikes on Hiroshima and Nagasaki that were to follow.

Meanwhile the huge Japanese merchant fleet, employed in
carrying vital oil and valuable minerals to the headquarters of an
empire singularly devoid of natural resources, had been steadily
blasted into extinction by the flashing torpedoes of the United
States Navy's submarines. Here indeed were the unsung heroes

of the splendid Pacific sea charge of three years' duration: four thousand miles from Pearl Harbor to the reef-rimmed slender long island of Okinawa. These men of "the silent service," as it was called, were fond of joking about how they had divided the Pacific between the enemy and themselves, conferring on Japan "the bottom half." In fact it was true. Only an occasional supply ship or transport arrived at or departed Nippon's numerous seaports, themselves silent, ghostly shambles. Incredibly, the American submarines, now out of sea targets, had penetrated Japan's inland seas to begin the systematic destruction of its ferry traffic. Transportation on the four Home Islands of Honshu, Shikoku, Kyushu, and Hokkaido was at a standstill. Little was moved: by road or rail, over the water or through the air. In the Imperial Palace hissing, bowing members of the household staff kept from Emperor Hirohito the shocking, grisly protests arriving in the daily mail: the index fingers of Japanese fathers who had lost too many sons to "the red-haired barbarians." Most of these doubters—silent and anonymous because they feared a visit from the War Lords' dreaded Thought Police—were men who had lived and worked in America, knowing it for the unrivaled industrial giant that it was. They did not share the general jubilation when "the emperor's glorious young eagles" arrived home from Pearl Harbor. Their hearts were filled with trepidation, with secret dread for the retribution that they knew would overtake their beloved country.

For eight months following Pearl Harbor, the victory fever had raged unchecked in Japan. During that time the striking power of America's Pacific Fleet had rolled with the tide on the floor of Battleship Row. Wake had fallen, Guam, the Philippines. The Rising Sun flew above the Dutch East Indies, it surmounted the French tricolor in Indochina, blotting out the Union Jack in Singapore, where columns of short tan men in mushroom helmets double-timed through silent streets. Burma and Malaya were also

Japanese. India's hundreds of millions were imperiled, great China was all but isolated from the world, Australia looked fearfully north to Japanese bases on New Guinea, toward the long double chain of the Solomon Islands drawn like two knives across its lifeline to America. But then, on August 7, 1942—exactly eight months after Vice Admiral Chuichi Nagomo had turned his aircraft carriers into the wind off Pearl Harbor—the American Marines landed on Guadalcanal and the counter-offensive had begun.

In Japan the war dance turned gradually into a dirge while doleful drums beat a requiem of retreat and defeat. Smiling Japanese mothers no longer strolled along the streets of Japanese towns and cities, grasping their "belts of a thousand stitches," entreating passersby to sew a stitch into these magical charms to be worn into battle by their soldier sons. For now those youths lay buried on faraway islands where admirals and generals—like the Melanesian or Micronesian natives whom they despised—escaped starvation by cultivating their own vegetable gardens of yams and sweet potatoes. And the belts that had failed to preserve the lives of the boys who wore them became battle souvenirs second only to the *Samurai* sabers of their fallen officers.

This, then, was the Japan that the United States Joint Chiefs of Staff still considered a formidable foe, so much so that it could be subdued only by an invasion force of a million men and thousands of ships, airplanes, and tanks. To achieve final victory, Okinawa was to be seized as a forward base for this enormous invading armada. In the fall of 1945 a three-pronged amphibious assault called Operation *Olympic* was to be mounted against southern Kyushu by the Sixth U.S. Army consisting of ten infantry divisions and three spearheading Marine divisions. This was to be followed in the spring of 1946 by Operation *Coronet*, a massive seaborne assault on the Tokyo Plain by the Eighth and Tenth Armies, spearheaded by another amphibious force of three Marine divisions and with the First Army transshipped from Europe to form a ten-division reserve. The entire operation would be under the command of General of the Armies MacArthur and Fleet Admiral Chester Nimitz.

Okinawa would be the catapult from which this mightiest amphibious assault force ever assembled would be hurled.

The Divine Wind

Japanese Imperial Headquarters, still refusing to believe that Nippon was beaten, still writing reports while wearing rose-colored glasses, also anticipated an inevitable and bloody fight for Okinawa as the prelude to a titanic struggle for Japan itself. While the American Joint Chiefs regarded Operation *Iceberg* as one more stepping-stone toward Japan, their enemy saw it as the anvil on which the hammer blows of a still-invincible Japan would destroy the American fleet.

Destruction of American sea power remained the chief objective of Japanese military policy. Sea power had brought the Americans through the island barriers that Imperial Headquarters had thought to be impenetrable, had landed them at Iwo within the very Prefecture of Tokyo, and now threatened to provide them a lodgment 385 miles closer to the Home Islands. Only sea power could make possible the invasion of Japan, something that had not happened in three thousand years of Japan's recorded history—something that had been attempted only twice before.

In 1274 and 1281 Kublai Khan, grandson of the great Genghis Khan and Mongol emperor of China, massed huge invasion

15

fleets on the Chinese coast for that purpose. Japan was unprepared to repel such stupendous armadas, but a *kamikaze*, or "Divine Wind"—actually a typhoon—struck both Mongol fleets, scattering and sinking them.

In early 1945, nearly seven centuries later, an entire host of Divine Winds came howling out of Nippon. They were the suicide bombers of the Special Attack Forces, the new *kamikaze* who had been so named because it was seriously believed that they too would destroy another invasion fleet.

They were the conception of Vice Admiral Takejiro Onishi. He had led a carrier group during the Battle of the Philippine Sea. After that Japanese aerial disaster known to the Americans as "the Marianas Turkey Shoot," Onishi had gone to Fleet Admiral Soemu Toyoda, commander of Japan's Combined Fleet, with the proposal to organize a group of flyers who would crash-dive loaded bombers onto the decks of American warships. Toyoda agreed. Like most Japanese he found the concept of suicide—so popular in Japan as a means of atonement for failure of any kind—a glorious method of defending the homeland. So Toyoda sent Onishi to the Philippines, where he began organizing *kamikaze* on a local and volunteer basis. Then came the American seizure of the Palaus and the Filipino invasion.

On October 15, 1944, Rear Admiral Masafumi Arima—the first *kamikaze*—tried to crash-dive the American carrier *Franklin*. He was shot down by Navy fighters, but Japanese Imperial Headquarters told the nation that he had succeeded in hitting the carrier—which he had not done—and thus "lit the fuse of the ardent wishes of his men."

The first organized attacks of the *kamikaze* came on October 25, at the beginning of the Battle of Leyte Gulf. Suicide bombers struck blows strong enough to startle the Americans and make them aware of a new weapon in the field against them, but not savage enough to shatter them. Too many *kamikaze* missed

their targets and crashed harmlessly into the ocean, too many lost
their way either arriving or returning, and too many were shot
down. Of 650 suiciders sent to the Philippines, only about a quarter of them scored hits—and almost exclusively on small ships
without the firepower to defend themselves like the cruisers, battleships, and aircraft carriers. But Imperial Headquarters, still
keeping the national mind carefully empty of news of failure, an-
nounced hits of almost 100 percent. Imperial Headquarters did
not believe its own propaganda, of course. Its generals and admirals privately guessed hits ranging from 12 to 50 percent, but
they also assumed that nothing but battleships and carriers had
been hit.

Thus was the *kamikaze* born, in an outburst of national ecstasy
and anticipated deliverance. In the homeland a huge corps of suiciders was organized under Vice Admiral Matome Ugaki. By January 1945 they were part of Japanese military strategy, if not the
dominant part. So many suiciders would be ordered out on an
operation, to be joined by so many first-class fighters and bombers: the fighters to clear the skies of enemy interceptors, the
bombers to ravage American shipping and guide the *kamikaze* to
their victims.

They needed to be guided because they usually were a com-
bination of old, stripped-down aircraft and young, often hopped-
up flyers. Admiral Ugaki did not use his newest planes or his most
skilled pilots, as Admiral Onishi had in the Philippines. Ugaki
considered this wasteful. He believed that the "spiritual power"
of the "glorious, incomparable young eagles" would compensate
for the missing firepower of obsolete crates from which even the
instruments had been removed. At a period in the Pacific War
when perceptive Japanese commanders were beginning to ridicule
the "bamboo-spear tactics" of the School of Spiritual Power, as
opposed to the realities of firepower, Ugaki was showering his
brave young volunteers—for brave they truly were—with enco-

miums of praise intended to silence whatever reservations they
may have had about piloting these patched-up old cripples, and
also to inspire the nation.

So the suiciders were hailed as saviors: wined, dined, photo-
graphed, lionized. Many of them attended their own funerals before taking off on their last mission. Farewell feasts were held in
their honor at the numerous airfields on the southernmost Japanese island of Kyushu. Solemn *Samurai* ceremonies were con-
ducted, and many toasts of *sake* drunk, so that some of the pilots
climbed aboard their airplanes on wobbly legs. It did not seem to
occur to the Japanese—and especially Ugaki—that insobriety
might affect the aim of the *kamikaze* and thus defeat the purpose
of the suicide corps; and this was because the concept of the
suicide-savior had so captivated the nation from schoolgirls to
Emperor Hirohito himself that the slightest word of criticism
would have been regarded as treason. And it was this very deep
and very real faith in another coming of a Divine Wind that dic-
tated to the planners at Imperial Headquarters exactly how the
battle of Okinawa was to be fought.

The speed with which the Americans were overrunning the Philippines had produced a mood of the blackest pessimism at
Imperial Headquarters in Tokyo in late 1944—until those roseate
reports of *kamikaze* success during December and January replaced the darkest despair with the brightest hopes. By 1945
Headquarters had decided that the United States would next
strike at Okinawa to seize a base for the invasion of Japan proper,
as the four Home Islands were called. It was now believed that
the *kamikaze* corps could greatly improve the chances for a successful defense of Okinawa, and thus perhaps—even probably—
prevent enemy landings in the Home Islands. So a plan called
Ten-Go, or "Heavenly Operation," was devised. New armies
were to be formed from a reserve of military-age men who had

been deferred for essential labor, while a powerful air force built around the *kamikaze* would be organized to destroy the Americans.

More than four thousand airplanes, both suicide and conventional, would launch an all-out attack, joined by hundreds of suicide motorboats operating from Okinawa and the Kerama Islands and followed by a suicide dash of Japan's remaining warships, including the mighty battleship *Yamato*. The air assaults would come from two directions: north from Formosa where the Japanese Army's Eighth Air Division and the Navy's First Air Fleet were based, and south from Kyushu, with a more powerful force combining several Army and Navy commands, all under the direction of Vice Admiral Ugaki. On February 6 a joint Army-Navy Air Agreement stated:

> In general Japanese air strength will be conserved until an enemy landing is underway or within the defense sphere . . . Primary emphasis will be laid on the speedy activation, training and mass employment of the Special Attack Forces (*kamikaze*) . . . The main target of Army aircraft will be enemy transports, and of Navy aircraft carrier attack forces.

On its face this was a bold plan conceived in an atmosphere of the most cordial cooperation. Actually, the only leaders motivated by the same conviction were those who believed that the war could no longer be won. Otherwise, there was a deep divergence: the Navy officers seeing *Ten-Go* as the last opportunity to score a great, redeeming victory; the Army staffers in agreement that the final battle would be fought not on Okinawa but on Kyushu. Though their views conflicted, their reasoning was logical: the sailors, certain that if airpower could not stop the enemy at Okinawa, neither would it do so on Kyushu; the Army insisting that even on the Philippines the Americans had not yet fought a major Japanese army, and that, shattered and whittled by the suicide-saviors, they could be repulsed in Japan proper. However, all—even the doubters—were convinced that at the very least a severe defeat must be inflicted on the Americans to compel the Allies to modify their demand for Unconditional Surrender.

There was one more consideration, probably more apparent to the Army than the Navy. Bamboo-spear tactics were out. The illogical belief that spiritual power could conquer firepower had spawned that other cause of Japan's absolute inability to halt the American charge across the Pacific: the doctrine of destroying the enemy invaders "at the water's edge." Those nocturnal, massed frontal attacks known as "Banzai charges" had repeatedly been broken in blood, leaving the Japanese defenders so weakened that they were powerless to resist. Now there was a new spirit informing the Japanese Army: defense in depth—as careful as the Banzai was reckless, as difficult for the enemy to overcome as the foolhardy wild Banzai had been easy for him to shatter, and so costly in the attrition of enemy men, machines, and ships as to weary the Americans and thus induce them to negotiate.

Ambush, or the tactics of delay raised to a military science, began on the large island of Biak off the western extremity of New Guinea. It was conceived by Colonel Kuzume Naoyuki, commander of about eleven thousand troops of the defense garrison there. Disdainful of the doctrine of destruction at the water's edge, he decided instead to allow the Americans to come ashore unopposed so that they would stroll unwarily into the trap he would prepare for them. This would turn the area around the vital airfield there into a martial honeycomb of caves and pillboxes—all mutually supportive—filled with riflemen, automatic weapons, artillery, batteries of mortars, and light tanks. Naoyuki also stockpiled these positions with enough ammunition, food, and water—that priceless liquid was less than abundant on Biak, where the heat and humidity would take a toll equal to enemy gunfire—to sustain his defense for months. Thus, when the 162nd Infantry of the Forty-first Division of the U.S. Army landed on Biak on May 27, 1944, they did indeed move confidently inland expecting little opposition—until they reached that vital airfield. Then, from the low-lying terrain around them and the ridges above, there fell a terrible storm of shot and shell that pinned them to the ground; it was not until dark that amtracks were able to extricate them from the trap.

Thereafter, there was no foolish and furious Banzai by which the Japanese enemy customarily bled itself to death. Biak was a grinding, shot-for-shot battle. Ambush, or delay, was repeated at Peleliu and Iwo Jima, battles that the U.S. Marines expected to be won within days or a week or so but lasted for months, with staggering losses not only in valuable time but in still more valuable life and equipment.

These were the tactics that Lieutenant General Mitsuru Ushijima intended to employ on Okinawa with his defending Japanese Thirty-second Army. After his arrival there in August 1944, he hurled himself into the gratifying task of turning that slender long island into an ocean fortress. In January 1945, he sent his chief of staff, Lieutenant General Isamu Cho, to Tokyo for a review of his defenses. Imperial Headquarters planners were delighted with his preparations, for they dovetailed with *Ten-Go.* Ushijima's monster ambush was just the tactic to lure the Americans within range of the suiciders—airborne and seaborne—to be smashed so shatteringly that the Thirty-second Army could take the offensive and destroy them.

Upon his return to Okinawa, Isamu Cho was a happy soldier, thirsting for battle and bursting to tell his chief the good news about Japan's devastating new weapon of the Divine Wind.

The Japanese *Samurai*

CHAPTER FOUR

To understand the *Samurai*—a hereditary class of professional warriors peculiar to Japan—it is necessary to understand the history of Nippon. Up until 1853, when the American Commodore Matthew Perry opened Japan to world trade, Nippon had been a hermit kingdom into which no foreigner who valued his life would venture. True, between the founding of the Island Empire in 660 B.C. and the arrival of Perry, there had been a brief interlude of intercourse with the West. This occurred after a storm drove a China-bound Portuguese ship ashore in 1543. Later ships brought Catholic missionaries, among them Saint Francis Xavier, the great Jesuit missionary and a leader of the Catholic Counter-Reformation, who stepped ashore in 1549. Under his influence the population of a large area of the southern island of Kyushu became Catholic Christians. This pleased neither the ruling shoguns (military commanders in chief who had seized power from the emperor) or the Buddhist priests.

The shoguns quite understandably suspected that the Catholic missionaries might actually be advance scouts or spies for the colonizing Catholic powers of Europe. They remembered that after Spanish priests came to the Philippines with Ferdinand Magellan, they were followed by Spanish soldiers who made those islands the possessions of the king of Spain. An uprising of Kyushu Christians was put down with ferocious severity, and in 1617 a persecution of Christians was begun. All Christians, whether foreign or Japanese—Protestant or Catholic—were hunted down ruthlessly, and those who did not recant under torture were executed.

Thereafter Japan sank back into isolation. No one could leave the country under pain of death, and no foreigner enter under the same grim penalty. Nor were oceangoing ships allowed to be built. Every Japanese family was required to register at a Buddhist temple, and interest in Buddhist studies was encouraged. Shinto, the naive nature-and-ancestor worship of ancient Japan, was also revived. Shinto, a Chinese word (significant of Chinese influence on Japanese culture), was based on a simple feeling of reverence for any surprising or awesome phenomenon of nature: a waterfall, a splendid cloud formation, a mountain, a magnificent tree, or even an oddly shaped stone. Places that stimulated such delight or awe became Shinto shrines. At the head of this basically shamanist religion stood a master medicine man: the divine emperor.

Japanese tradition claimed that the imperial family was directly descended from the sun goddess. Actually, this family issued from the Yamato clan, which claimed the sun goddess as its progenitor. During the third and fourth centuries the Yamato clan's priest-chiefs gained suzerainty and may be said to have unified the country, although without destroying the rights of the other clans. This ruling family, then, could claim an antiquity with which none of the other reigning families of the world could compare. It also could claim the allegiance of its subjects unto death itself. To fail or embarrass the emperor was a heinous, unforgivable crime for which there could be no penance or expiation other than self-destruction. This belief in the divinity of the emperor was cleverly and cynically exploited by the shoguns, who ruled the country through the emperor as figurehead.

The shoguns came to power after the imperial armies in the eighth century suffered setbacks at the hands of Japan's original inhabitants, the Ainu—an extremely hairy race thereafter exiled to the inhospitable North by the heartless and frequently hairless Japanese, and called in contempt "the hairy Ainu." Scorning the imperial conscripts, the shoguns formed their own smaller but better trained and disciplined armies. These were commanded by a new class of officers drawn from the sons of local clan chiefs and called *Samurai*. They formed this new hereditary class of professional warriors serving the *daimyos*, or feudal lords.

The *Samurai* were distinguished by their hair, shaven in front and top-knotted, and the clan badge worn on their kimonos. They lived Spartan lives and were rigidly drilled—from childhood to manhood—in self-control: a *Samurai* was taught to show "no joy or anger." Nor was he ever to engage in trade or handle money. Like Christian seminarians, he had contempt for commerce as being *infra dignitatem*, beneath his dignity. He was also trained to excel in the martial arts. Indeed the two swords worn by the *Samurai*—one long and one short—were also badges of rank. *Samurai* were expected to become especially proficient with the long, two-handed sword, actually a thick, heavy, single-edged, and extremely sharp saber. The short one was for decapitating a fallen enemy or dispatching himself by *seppuku*, more commonly known as *hara-kiri*, literally, "stomach cutting." To kill himself in atonement for failure or disgrace, a *Samurai* would squat on the floor and thrust his short sword into his stomach—turning it in a ceremonial disembowelment that, if it became unbearably painful, could be ended by a comrade standing by to strike his neck with a saber, severing the spinal column.

A lifetime of cultivating indifference to pain, however, was part of a *Samurai*'s code of *Bushido*: "the way of the warrior."

With this inevitably arrogant warrior class, permitted to cut down any commoner "who has behaved to him in a manner other than he expected," the shoguns ruled Japan. And their reign continued for more than two centuries after the extinction of Christianity. It ended only when Commodore Perry appeared in his steam-driven "black ships," so terrifying to the insular Japanese when they saw these vessels without sails moving easily against the wind on Tokyo Bay. Very quickly a treaty opening two ports to the Americans was signed.

This unprecedented deference (not to say obeisance) to a foreign power so enraged conservatives of all callings—the merchants, *daimyos*, the *Samurai*—that it provoked a revolution known as the Meiji Restoration ending the power of the shoguns and restoring it to the emperor. It also culminated the career of the *Samurai*. No ruler could feel entirely safe with such dangerous zealots at large within his borders, and so by imperial edict these fierce warriors accepted the lump-sum termination offered them to hang up their swords and become merchants, lawyers, doctors, or bureaucrats. But they did not remain long suppressed, for the Meiji Restoration, in perhaps the most astonishing national turnabout in history, had embraced in one swoop the entire apparatus of the once-despised Western civilization. Everything invented or developed by the "Round Eyes" since Greece, Rome, and the advent of the Christian Era—their science, industry, culture, political institutions, methods of education, business practices, economics, dress, and even sports—was swallowed whole by Nippon.

Despite the undoubted exuberance of this nonviolent social revolution (sometimes comical to a Westerner at first sight of a smaller Japanese going to his daily workplace in a tuxedo hanging on him like a scarecrow's suit and a top hat reaching down to his ears), the change was outward only; Japan, for all of its pretensions to democracy, remained a paternalistic, authoritarian state. The secret police organized in the 1600s may have been banned, but the new Japan replaced them with Thought Police, censors and spies sniffing out sedition and "suspicious" activity like tireless bloodhounds, and empowered like the *Samurai* of old to put to death anyone caught doing "anything different." In classrooms and army barracks young Japanese were taught to glory in Nippon's military traditions, to believe that dying on the battlefield for the emperor was the most sublime fate to which a man could aspire.

Inevitably the spirit of the *Samurai* returned and their code of *Bushido* was revived. Soldiers of a mainly peasant army, both officers and men, were trained in the hard, selfless *Samurai* school, taught to think of themselves as heirs of that departed warrior class. Officers adopted a so-called *Samurai* saber, much like the two-handed long sword of old, as their badge of rank. Properly sharpened and even though wielded by diminutive Japanese, it could sever a prisoner's head at a single stroke, and this summary execution of captives—usually after they had been tortured for information—became one of the least gruesome features of Japan's new, *Samurai*-led army as it took the field in pursuit of territorial conquest and the raw materials and markets in which Nippon, for a modern industrial nation, was so deplorably deficient. Eventually the chief officers among them emerged as the War Lords of Japan. In collusion with the *zaibatsu*—leading politicians, bureaucrats, and industrialists such as the Mitsubishi and Mitsui families—the War Lords ruled the country through the figurehead of Hirohito.

This career of territorial aggrandizement by an authoritarian coalition began in 1879 with Nippon's annexation of the Ryukyu Islands, of which Okinawa was the largest. Sixty-six years later three typical *Samurai* took charge of defending this last barrier between American armed forces and the Home Islands of Japan.

———

Lieutenant General Mitsuru Ushijima—commander of the Japanese Thirty-second Army—may be said to have been the *Samurai* beau ideal. Ramrod-straight and lean, sharp-featured with a graying military brush mustache, he was able to awe subordinates by his unshakable composure and iron self-control. Yet he was a considerate man whose staff not only respected but even revered him. Ushijima's style was low-key. He abstained from the rough-and-tumble of staff discussions of policy, plans, or operations; in which, as had happened during the Guadalcanal disaster, irate officers could actually come to blows. Rather, he let his aides make the decisions, which he would either approve or reject. But he always took responsibility for the results, good or bad. In their unreserved admiration of him, his idolizing staff compared him to Takamori Saigo, a celebrated hero of the Meiji Restoration.

Early in the war Ushijima had distinguished himself as an infantry group commander during the conquest of Burma. There he met Isamu Cho, chief of staff of the Southern Army. They returned to Tokyo together, Ushijima to become commandant of the Japanese Military Academy, Cho to serve on the General Military Affairs Bureau. They also came to Okinawa together, Ushijima as the Thirty-second's chief, Cho as his chief of staff—and no two men could differ more in character.

Ushijima the serene was a man of presence, capable of inspiring his subordinates. He also possessed the rare gift of seeing his own incapacities, which he filled by choosing Major General Cho, a firebrand and a planner and organizer, strict but resourceful, aggressive, and so invincibly explosive in argument as to be unpopular. Deceptively scholarly-looking with thick wide spectacles that exaggerated his owlish features, he was actually—in contrast to the Spartan, abstemious Ushijima—a bon vivant. In his quarters, even toward the end of the battle for Okinawa, might be found unrivaled meals, the best Scotch whiskey, the finest *sake*, and the prettiest women. The burly Cho was also something of a bully, and the young officers who served him resented his hectoring tirades, even though they admitted that he could make them work harder than any other officer.

Isamu Cho had risen at fifty-one to the rank of lieutenant general and was in line for another star. In 1930, while a captain, he had joined the *Sakura-kai*, or "Cherry Society," whose hundred-odd members—all firebrands like Cho—were sworn to cleanse Japan of all Western influences that they considered inimical to the ancient virtues of the *Samurai*. Antidemocratic and anticapitalist, they sought to establish a military dictatorship and had chosen the cherry tree as their emblem because its brilliant though short-lived blossoms symbolized the warrior *Samurai*'s readiness to die for the emperor at any moment.

A few generals eager to wear the dictatorial mantle courted the Cherry favor, and thus contributed to the society's increasing influence and to Cho's emergence as the leading hothead and strong-arm advocate. In January 1931, he helped plot a conspiracy to murder the prime minister and replace him with a leading general, but that distinguished officer declined to accept the honor, since he seems to have expected to gain that eminence by legal means. In October the Cherries tried again, with Cho once more the leader. The plan was to have revolutionaries fly over Tokyo to bomb selected targets, chief among them the prime minister's residence. With him dead, Emperor Hirohito could be compelled to choose a general as his successor. However, Cho's very exuberance foiled the plot. At one of the meetings, held in a geisha house in Tokyo's red-light district, he declared that the conspiracy must succeed "even if it is necessary to threaten the emperor with a drawn dagger." To one Cherry member this was treasonous talk indeed, and after he blew the whistle, Japanese military police raided a geisha house to arrest the ringleaders— Cho not included—and put an end to the notorious plot of "the Brocade Banner."

In any other army Cho's activity would at least have led to his being court-martialed or even executed, but instead of being punished he was rewarded with a coveted assignment to the Kwantung Army, then engaged in ripping the province of Manchuria from the flabby big body of the Chinese giant. Nor was the public as outraged as it might have been by the Brocade Banner affair, for in those days a man who excused his misdeeds by wrapping himself in the flag of patriotism was forgiven almost anything. Gradually, however, as the militarists tightened their hold on Japan, any kind of opposition to the status quo, no matter how supposedly patriotic, was not so conveniently ignored.

Nevertheless Cho did not—could not—restrain himself. In 1938 he nearly provoked a war between Japan and the Soviet Union when he and another officer ordered an unauthorized attack on Russian forces just over the Manchurian border. Three years later, as chief of staff of the army that had seized Thailand, he seems to have encouraged hostilities between Thai and Vichy French troops. Yet, he remained in the high command's mystifyingly good graces, much to the dismay of generals senior to him who also sought the Okinawa assignment. Perhaps Imperial Headquarters believed that Cho's very excess of zeal could now be helpful rather than detrimental to the army. If the fires burning in his breast could rekindle the ardor of the soldiers on Okinawa, then another kind of *kamikaze* might yet overwhelm superior American firepower and save Japan.

Such a possibility might indeed have inhabited the minds of these mystical Japanese generals and admirals, men who actually did believe that the soul of a *Samurai* killed fighting for the emperor would dwell eternally in Yasakuni Shrine in Tokyo. But from the standpoint of reality, a more hopeful savior than either the traditionalist Ushijima or the fiery Cho existed in the person of Colonel Hiromichi Yahara, chief planning officer of the Thirty-second Army.

At forty-two Yahara was much younger than either Ushijima or Cho, although his record was almost as impressive. Graduated from the Japanese Military Academy in the class of 1923, Yahara had served in an infantry regiment, had attended the Japanese War College and spent ten months at Fort Moultrie in the United States as an exchange officer. He had also served with distinction during fighting in China, Thailand, Malaya, and Burma. Tall for a Japanese, poised, patrician, an intellectual, there was about him a kind of superciliousness—probably born of his contempt for those advocates of bamboo-spear tactics—that alienated many of his comrades. Especially Cho. Indeed, Cho and Yahara were as antithetical as two men could be. Where Cho was impetuous, Yahara was deliberate; where Cho was physical and aggressive, Yahara was thoughtful and careful; and where Cho was all heart, Yahara was all head. To Yahara war was not a contest but a science, to be won by superior tactics adjusted to terrain, weapons, and troops, not by those wretchedly bloody Banzai charges. In this intellectualism and the aloofness issuing from it, and in his unconcealed contempt for others who did not share his acumen, he again offended fellow officers on Ushijima's staff.

Nevertheless Hiromichi Yahara's rationalism was the perfect complement to Ushijima's magnetism and Cho's fire, thus conferring on the Thirty-second Army a superb leadership, which—now devoted to the new tactic of defense in depth to be executed on the most compatible terrain imaginable—did not presage a quick and easy victory for the American invaders. This trio's intention to give up no ground willingly and to whittle and weary the enemy was reflected in the Thirty-second Army's slogan composed by Ushijima:

One Plane for One Warship
One Boat for One Ship
One Man for Ten of the Enemy or One Tank

Fulfillment of the first slogan was up to the *kamikaze,* for General Ushijima had little airpower based on Okinawa's five airfields.

"One Boat for One Ship" would be the objective by nautical Divine Winds of the Sea Raiding Squadrons. They were enlisted youths fresh out of high school, trained to ram explosive-stuffed motorboats into American ships. There were about 700 suicide boats hidden in the Ryukyus, and approximately 350 were only about fifteen miles west of southern Okinawa in the islets of the Kerama-retto.

The third stricture was left to a force of about one hundred thousand men, of whom a fifth were conscripted from the Okinawan population. The bulk of these troops was concentrated in Okinawa's southern third.

Here Ushijima began to build a line facing north like a broad arrowhead. Its point rested on the heights surrounding Shuri and Shuri Castle, the city and citadel of Okinawa's ancient kings. Its flanks swept back to the sea on either side, through a jungle of ridges to the chief city of Naha on the left (to the west), through similar hills back to Yonabaru Airfield on the right. It was the Naha-Shuri-Yonabaru line. It held the bulk of Ushijima's fighting men—the Sixty-second Division, which had served in China, the Twenty-fourth Division, and the Forty-fourth Independent Mixed Brigade. To its left, on Oroku Peninsula jutting into the sea west of Naha, were about thirty-five hundred Japanese sailors and seven thousand Japanese civilians under Vice Admiral Minoru Ota. Roughly three thousand soldiers of the Second Infantry Unit under Colonel Takehiko Udo held the wild, uninhabited northern half of Okinawa—that part that Ushijima, at the urging of Yahara, had chosen not to defend. Nor would Ushijima attempt to contest the Hagushi Beaches in west-central Okinawa. He would defend the Minatoga Beaches to the south because they were in the rear of his Naha-Shuri-Yonabaru line, but he would protect almost nothing north of that line, except, of course, its approaches. He would not even defend Yontan and Kadena Airfields to the east of the Hagushi Beaches. These would be wrecked the moment the Americans appeared by a special force drawn from the *Boeitai*, the Home Guard of about twenty thousand men whom Ushijima had ruthlessly called up from among the Okinawan males between twenty and forty. The wrecking crew was called the *Bimbo Butai*, or "Poor Detachment," by those Japanese soldiers whose loathing of Okinawa and all things Okinawan had already become a problem to General Ushijima.

Conscription of the *Boeitai* had unwittingly led to one of the chief complaints among Ushijima's soldiers: the lack of fresh vegetables. There hadn't been enough adult males around to produce the normal vegetable crop that fall and winter, and Tokyo was shipping in bullets, not beans.

"I cannot bear having just a cup of rice for a meal with no side dishes at all," a soldier wrote. "Our health will be ruined."

The lament was raised frequently elsewhere, and Ushijima took account of it by urging his men to "display a more firm and resolute spirit, hold to the belief of positive victory, and always remember the spirit of martyrdom and of dying for the good of the country."

By way of consolation, the general issued each man a pint and a half of sweet-potato brandy, proclaimed a temporary amnesty for drunkards, and promised another issue on April 29, 1945, when the Emperor Hirohito would become forty-four years old.

Cho came back from his visit to Tokyo in late January. He reported that Ushijima's defense plans dovetailed with Imperial Headquarters strategy and that he had been able to dispel some doubts about the decision not to defend the Hagushi Beaches. Cho was also elated by a secret report he had seen concerning the *kamikaze*. The attacks by twenty-six of Admiral Ugaki's six-plane units had brought about instantaneous sinking of one American battleship, six carriers, and thirty-four cruisers. Even the clearheaded Cho had been blown overboard by the Divine Wind. He got out an inspirational message for the Thirty-second Army's top commanders. It said:

The brave ruddy-faced warriors with white silken scarves tied about their heads, at peace in their favorite planes, dash out spiritedly to the attack. The skies are slowly brightening.

But the skies were rather darkening with the airplanes of the American Fast Carrier Forces, which began striking the Great Loo Choo late that month. After the raid of January 22, a Japanese soldier wrote in his diary:

While some of the planes fly overhead and strafe, the big bastards fly over the airfield and drop bombs. The ferocity of the bombing is terrific. It really makes me furious. It is past three o'clock and the raid is still on. At six the last two planes brought the raid to a close. What the hell kind of bastards are they? Bomb from six to six!

They were "hard-nosed bastards," these Americans, and there were more and bigger ones coming—toward both the Ryukyus and Japan, both by air and by sea. Naha was being pounded to rubble and the wolf packs of the American submarine service were littering the floor of the China Sea with sunken cargo vessels and drowned soldiers.

The most shocking loss of all occurred on June 29, 1944, when the U.S. submarine *Sturgeon* under Lieutenant Commander C. L. Murphy sent four torpedoes flashing into the side of the troop transport *Toyama Maru*, sending her to the bottom along with fifty-six hundred soldiers and most of her officers and crew.

Such reports helped to discourage the troops of the Thirty-second Army, and one private wrote in his diary: "The enemy is brazenly planning to destroy completely every last ship, cut our supply lines and attack us."

He was absolutely correct, and "the enemy" by then was also hurling neutralizing thunderbolts at the homeland.

Throughout February and March, while the Marines were

conquering Iwo Jima, land- and carrier-based planes struck again
and again at the Great Loo Choo. Superforts began to rage all
over the Ryukyus. Okinawa was effectively cut off from Kyushu
in the north, Formosa in the south. On March 1, while the Fast
Carrier Forces were returning to Ulithi from their third strike at
Japan, there were so many planes strafing, bombing, and rocketing Okinawa that pilots had to get in line for a crack at a target.
Lieutenant General Mitsuru Ushijima was impressed.

"You cannot regard the enemy as on a par with you," he told
his men. "You must realize that material power usually overcomes
spiritual power in the present war. The enemy is clearly our superior in machines. Do not depend on your spirits overcoming
this enemy. Devise combat method [*sic*] based on mathematical
precision—then think about displaying your spiritual power."

Ushijima's order was perhaps the most honest issued by a
Japanese commander throughout the war. It was *Bushido* revised,
turned upside down and inside out—but the revision had been
made too late.

First Blood for America

In early October 1944—little more than a week after the crucial San Francisco conference—Fleet Admiral Bull Halsey's monster Task Force Thirty-eight was speeding blacked-out through the Pacific night, bound northwestward for the opening salvos of the Okinawa campaign. When dawn broke it revealed a splendid and thrilling spectacle: seventeen aircraft carriers carrying one thousand aircraft, six fast battleships, fourteen cruisers, and fifty-eight destroyers together with the subsidiary ships such as oilers and tenders plunging through a white-capped gray sea almost at flank speed, some of them with "a bone in their teeth"—white bow waves curving away from either side of their prows—a huge and terrifying force to any Japanese unfortunate enough to witness their approach. Actually, Halsey's fleet alone was more powerful than the entire battle force deployed by Admiral Nimitz at Midway on June 6, 1942, to defeat Admiral Isoroku Yamamoto's Combined Fleet, thus restoring carrier power in the Pacific to par with five apiece and—more important—turning the tide of naval battle against Japan.

Halsey's TF 38 was so large that it was spread out into four separate groups, each a task force in itself with a rear admiral in command. The precious carriers, as always, sailed in the center of each group in boxlike formation, with the battleships and cruisers steaming at the quarters, their protective antiaircraft guns raised like spikes fingering the sky. Around each formation sped the circling destroyers, seagoing sheep dogs snapping at the heels of their flocks, but actually screening them and searching, searching, searching for enemy submarines.

On all ships, surface and air radars rotated unceasingly, feeding information to their Combat Information Centers, each vessel's nerve center where sailors worked silently in darkened compartments below. On the bridges or in sea cabins immediately adjacent to them stood the ship captains and task group commanders, tense and with furrowed brows anticipating—while dreading—those sudden emergencies that arise swiftly and require instant reaction. Throughout TF 38 hundreds of men perched high on the crow's nests of masts swept the sea with binoculars, looking for those telltale tips of periscopes cutting through the water, and thus supplementing the electrical impulses of the radar or the pinging of the sonar sniffing out strangers submerged beneath the waves.

Day after day as the carriers penetrated deeper and deeper into enemy waters, they were turned into the wind to launch planes, either for antisubmarine or defensive fighter patrols. As they were catapulted into the air, the destroyers on pilot-rescue duty churned closer to either side of the flattops. It was the "tin cans'" duty to rescue crashed pilots. Aboard these slender long "black-water ships," always a thrilling sight with their sterns dug into the water and their prows high, sometimes even bouncing on the waves, throwing up huge plumes of white spray, the deck officers kept a worried eye on the carriers' deck angle. If a flattop in a changing wind turned suddenly to keep it on its bow, the destroyer might ram the carrier. To prevent such disaster, deck officers—usually young and highly responsible sailors—were carefully screened and trained.

Each carrier had a dual organization, its regular crew that sailed or fought the ship and its air group. The air group maintained and flew the planes: about eighty in the big *Essex* class twenty-seven-thousand-ton flattops, forty in the smaller *Independence* class, a carrier with flight decks mounted on a cruiser's hull. With Vice Admiral Marc Mitscher in tactical command, TF 38's airplanes—those peerless Curtiss Helldiver dive-bombers and Grumman Avenger torpedo planes, Grumman Hellcat fighter-bombers and fighters—would scourge Okinawa land and sea, especially the enemy island's three operational airfields as well as the one on little Ie Island off Okinawa's midwestern shore. All facilities—runways, barracks, warehouses, hangars, AA (antiaircraft) defenses, parked planes—would be blasted. Perhaps just as important, camera planes would take mosaic strip photographs of the island for map-makers back in Hawaii.

Before dawn of October 10, 1944, while intelligence officers briefed air crews on Okinawa's defenses, all seventeen of the flattops made ready for battle. Elevators brought planes topside to be stationed in rows on teakwood decks awaiting launch or takeoff. Below, armorers armed the planes with bombs, five-inch rockets, twenty-one-inch torpedoes, or belts of .50 caliber machine-gun ammunition. At dawn pilot-rescue destroyers took station. With an ear-piercing *swooosh!* bow catapults hurled aloft those planes that needed artificial momentum while others roared down the deck to become airborne themselves.

Between daybreak and dusk the American airmen flew 1,396 sorties over Okinawa, dropping more than five hundred tons of bombs, destroying suicide submarines, flaming enemy fighters, sinking a tender, smaller ships, and the power-driven fishing boats in Naha harbor, while setting that city of sixty-five thousand persons ablaze. In all, ten transports and thirty merchant ships went to the bottom, along with half of the power-driven fishing boats and sixteen smaller warships—a serious loss of Okinawa's patrol boats and trawlers assigned to supplying the island.

Perhaps more serious were the attacks on Naha warehouses, where three hundred thousand sacks of rice—enough to feed the Thirty-second Army for a month—were burned, plus the loss of five million rounds of rifle and machine-gun ammunition, ten thousand rounds of light artillery and mortar shells, and four hundred rounds of 47 mm antitank ammunition. The exact number of enemy planes destroyed or damaged was not known. One Japanese general was killed and another wounded, while military deaths totaled two hundred. Among civilians five hundred persons died—a tragic loss, even though unintended. Eventually, however, the Okinawans would understand that the safest place for them during such attacks—which they called "typhoons of steel"—was within Okinawa's numerous caves, which sheltered them during the real typhoons that scourged the island. Perhaps even more important than the damage dealt to Ushijima's installations were the thousands of aerial photographs taken, which, with others shot earlier by B-29s flying from China, enabled the American map-makers in Hawaii to produce a fairly accurate 1:24,000-scale map of utmost value to both infantry and artillery.

Halsey's losses, meanwhile, were minimal: five pilots and four crewmen carried as missing in action and twenty-one planes lost. Upon the approach of night, Halsey reversed course, speeding southward again to strike Formosa, confident that before Okinawa's cratered airfields could be repaired and replacement planes flown in, TF 38 could complete its mission without intervention from the Great Loo Choo.

Kamikaze Strike/
Franklin's Ordeal

CHAPTER SIX

In the middle of March the planning stages for Operation *Iceberg* came to an end and the preinvasion bombardment intended to soften up Okinawa for the attack began. Now Task Force Fifty-eight under Admiral Spruance sortied from its anchorage at Ulithi for the first phase of destroying enemy airpower based on Kyushu.

Spruance's fast carriers could not have appeared at a more difficult time for Admiral Ugaki. Preparations for *Ten-Go* were not complete, and even if they had been, the Heavenly Operation's prime targets were to be comparatively defenseless troop transports and supply ships—not those seventeen dreadful American flattops with their thousand airplanes, those half-dozen big battleships, those fourteen cruisers—all of which could fight back. Only the Fifth Air Japanese Fleet was ready for action, and of its eight air groups two were strictly one-way suiciders. Even these heroic *kamikaze* had been so few hours in the air that they still had difficulty landing their planes. Kyushu's fifty-five airfields had not yet been made ready for the anticipated raids, although Ugaki's engineers were tunneling into the hills to shelter pilots, troops, ordnance, and repair facilities, while camouflaging run-

ways and littering abandoned fields with dummies and useless aircraft. Communications were poor—as they usually were among
the Japanese—and there were real problems in transmitting orders from Ugaki's headquarters at Kanoya. Poor mechanical com-
munication inhibited Japanese battle coordination throughout the
war, but even worse was the consistent failure to report defeat,
perhaps because to do so would require the unfortunate commander to kill himself. Probably the worst instance of this
peculiarly Japanese weakness was after the Battle of Midway. Admiral Yamamoto never told the Army he had lost four carriers
there; although he informed Premier Hideki Tojo he had been
defeated, he never supplied the details. Emperor Hirohito heard
nothing. On a much smaller scale, but perhaps even more shocking, was the report to Tokyo Headquarters of the complete annihilation of the two-thousand-man Ichiki Detachment by the
Second Battalion, First Marines, on Guadalcanal. All that was revealed was that "the attack of the Ichiki Detachment was not
entirely successful." Japan's unique ideographic language was another cause of imprecise orders. Finally, the acrimonious debates
that could divide staff planners at every level was one more hin-
drance; such a furor arose at Imperial Headquarters over whether
or not to use the Special Attack Forces against Spruance's approaching fleet.

One side was against expending the *kamikaze* against enemy
warships when the true purpose of *Ten-Go* was to destroy as many
troop transports and supply ships as possible, while the opposing
group argued that a passive defense on Kyushu would expose the
island to such destruction from sea and sky that there wouldn't
be any aircraft left to strike TF 58. In the end, Tokyo ordered
Ugaki to hit Spruance with what he had.

He did. From the start of the American attack at 5:45 A.M.
on March 18 and throughout the following day Ugaki hurled
193 planes—including 69 *kamikaze*—at the Americans again attacking in four separate carrier groups. Of these, 161 planes—or

83 percent—were lost, while another 50 planes were damaged on the ground. Even with such staggering losses Admiral Ugaki was gratified, for his pilots—again retrieving victory from defeat with a few strokes of the pen, and for whom all minnows were whales during those two days—had reported hitting five carriers, two battleships, three cruisers, and one unidentified ship. But they reported these "losses" with such joyful shouts of victory that Ugaki assumed that they were all sunk, and that Spruance had withdrawn because his fleet was so badly crippled that the Okinawa invasion would be postponed for some time.

Actually, TF 58—though shaken—was far from being crippled. Japanese bombers had indeed scored hits, damaging four big carriers: *Wasp* seriously and *Franklin* so badly that she was presumed lost. It was at exactly 7:08 A.M. on March 19 that *Franklin*'s ordeal began. At that moment a lone Judy* bomber undetected by radar emerged from a low overcast to drop two 550-pound bombs from only a hundred feet above the flattop's wooden flight deck. The first missile pierced the deck just ahead of a pair of Helldiver bombers, while the second penetrated aft among a group of twenty-nine fueled and armed Helldivers, Avengers, and Corsairs awaiting their turn to be launched. Zooming up and away from the double explosions' flame and shock waves, the Judy was unharmed by the fusillade of shells fired at her by the carrier's AA gunners, but was shot down by Commander E. B. Parker, chief of *Franklin*'s air group. But its destruction was small compensation for the dreadful damage it had inflicted on the carrier.

Both bombs exploded in the hangar deck, setting afire twenty-three planes, fueled, armed, and awaiting their turn to be moved by elevator to the flight deck above. Flames and explosives flashing from the stricken planes instantly killed most of a line of about

---

* Japanese warplanes were divided into feminine names for bombers and masculine ones for fighters.

two hundred sailors and airmen waiting to descend to the mess deck below for breakfast. Almost simultaneously a huge and growing cloud of black smoke enveloped *Franklin*, obscuring her from the sight of surrounding ships.

On the navigation bridge concussions struck *Franklin*'s skipper, Captain Leslie Gehres, knocking him sprawling. Jumping erect, he was horrified to see "a sheet of flame come out from under the starboard side of the flight deck" engulfing the starboard batteries and spreading aft. At the same instant, Gehres saw that "a great column of flame and black smoke came out from the forward elevator well." To clear the smoke and flame from his ship, he ordered Quartermaster V. R. Ryan to steer *Franklin* to the right. Ryan did, but succeeded in surrounding the entire "island" superstructure—himself and the skipper included—in a cloud of hot, oily smoke issuing from the parked planes burning aft. Realizing that his ship was also stricken in its stern, Gehres ordered Ryan to swing the carrier the other way, meanwhile ordering the still-functioning engine room to increase speed by two-thirds. Almost at once the scorching smoke was blown clear of *Franklin*.

Now there ensued a spate of morning-long blasts, mostly from bombs and Tiny Tim twelve-inch rockets stored on deck. The Tiny Tim were especially frightening to men trying to fight the flames, because, as Commander Joe Taylor, the ship's executive, later described it, "Some screamed by the bridge to starboard, some to port and some straight up the flight deck." Yet, even in the midst of this death-dealing holocaust, neither Gehres nor Taylor lost their sense of humor. "Joe," Gehres said when he saw Parker approaching, "I'll have to say the same thing the admiral told you when you were last bombed: your face is dirty as hell!"

Grinning, the knot in his stomach quickly coming undone, Parker hurried to the flight deck to organize fire-fighting parties. From there he hastened to the hangar deck to organize the same details. Because foam and CO_2 were useless to squelch the inferno raging on *Franklin*'s decks, a pair of emergency pumps began supplying salt water to the fire hoses now put into play. Meanwhile, hundreds of sailors and airmen trapped by the flames took the only recourse possible to save themselves: they jumped overboard to a man, until there were long strings of heads bobbing on either side of the carrier. While *Franklin* pulled ahead of the swimmers at a steady eight knots, pilot-rescue destroyers closed her stern to pick up the survivors. Eventually they rescued hundreds.

Both to Captain Gehres and Rear Admiral R. E. Davison, commander of Task Group 58.2, it was clear that *Franklin* was badly hurt and might go under. To continue to direct his ships and planes against the enemy, Davison had no other choice but to remove his flag to another ship. But as he prepared to board the light cruiser *Santa Fe*, which he had ordered to come alongside the blazing *Franklin* to help fight fires and take off wounded, he was pleased to hear Gehres flatly reject any proposal to abandon ship. Gehres knew that perhaps three hundred of his men were trapped below in a mess compartment beneath the blazing hangar deck. "I had promised these kids I'd get them out," he explained. Meanwhile, Dr. J. L. Fuelling, a ship's physician, calmed the trapped sailors by ordering them to sit quietly and not consume oxygen by talking. As they sat terrified—who would not be?—in the stifling heat, the only air reaching them came from a hole in the ship's side just big enough to pass a baseball through. It is probable that they might have suffocated if not rescued soon, and that succor did come from a brave junior-grade lieutenant named Donald Cary.

As ship's fuel and water officer, Cary was familiar with the maze of passageways and compartments belowdecks, and he relied upon this knowledge to grope his way to locate the trapped bluejackets and lead them topside to safety—a daring feat for which he received a Medal of Honor.

That highest military award in the gift of the United States also went to Chaplain Joseph O'Callahan. To Commander Stephen Jurka, *Franklin*'s navigator, Father O'Callahan was "a soul-stirring sight. He seemed to be everywhere, giving Extreme Unction to the dead and dying, urging the men on and himself handling hoses, jettisoning ammunition and doing everything he could to save the ship." He seemed as composed as his Master moving through the smoke with the cross on his helmet shining like a beacon, "his head bowed slightly as if in meditation or prayer." Marveling at his serenity, Captain Gehres said: "I never saw a man so completely disregard the danger of being killed . . ."

Perhaps the most awesome feat of seamanship during *Franklin*'s entire ordeal came from Captain Hal Fitz of the *Santa Fe*, who daringly slammed into the carrier's side, remaining there to fight fires and take off wounded as well as able sailors. In spite of continuing explosions like strings of giant firecrackers, Fitz doggedly held *Santa Fe* fast, his own hoses joining *Franklin*'s in dousing flames, meanwhile taking aboard eight hundred of the carrier's seamen.

By noon the fires were dying down and the explosions less frequent and dangerous. But *Franklin* was still dead in the water, her black gangs having been driven from the engine rooms by intense heat. Commandeering a pickup force of messmen, Commander Taylor successfully seized a towline from the heavy cruiser *Pittsburgh* and began a crawling withdrawal from Japanese waters at a limping speed of six knots. That night a special detail equipped with breathing apparatus reduced *Franklin*'s dangerous list of thirty degrees while a party of daring volunteers braved smoke and heat to enter a boiler room and relight a pair of boilers. *Franklin* began to move under its own power.

The next day, with six boilers operating, the carrier dropped the *Pittsburgh* tow and went cleaving through the waves at a spanking fifteen knots. But then, in early afternoon, hearts breathing free at last constricted in fear again when another bold Judy bomber came gliding out of the sun. Without power to operate the flattop's plentiful AA guns, *Franklin* appeared helpless—until another crew of volunteers wrestled a heavy quadruple 40 mm gun mount around and fired it so accurately that the Judy was forced to nose upward at its release point, and its bombs—almost grazing the carrier—exploded harmlessly in the sea about two hundred feet from the ship.

Soon *Franklin* was out of the impact area. Captain Gehres now took stock of his human losses. He was shocked to find that 724 of his men had been killed and another 1,428 either wounded or unavailable and presumed to be aboard the five destroyers and two cruisers assigned to rescue duty. But there were still 103 officers and 603 enlisted men present able to sail the ship, although many of them were still in shock. Rather than have many more succumb to the paralysis of combat fatigue, Gehres wisely instituted a program of punishing and distracting work: burying their fallen comrades at sea, clearing the decks of wreckage, and scouring blackened compartments. By the time *Franklin* reached Pearl Harbor, those who saw her decks looking like "a shredded wheat biscuit" were amazed that she had survived the four-thousand-mile voyage back to base; and when her anchors went clattering down the hawse pipes off New York's Brooklyn Navy Yard she looked "almost presentable." In truth, because of her gallant skipper and crew, *Franklin* was by far the most shattered carrier on either side to survive its ordeal.

With *Wasp* and *Franklin* out of action, Admiral Spruance at once reduced his striking strength to three groups, distributing his remaining vessels among them, after which—with a few farewell sweeps over still-numbed and battered Kyushu—he retired far out to sea to refuel. Spruance's flyers claimed a total of five hundred enemy planes destroyed, three hundred shot down in air battles: an estimate that seems exaggerated. Still, they had certainly decimated Admiral Ugaki's *Ten-Go* force, leaving him with about thirty-six hundred of his original command of four thousand planes. Worse were his losses in skilled pilots. And he had not, as he had judged from his aviators' wildly optimistic reports of enemy ships sunk, in any way delayed the invasion of Okinawa.

The "Americans"

CHAPTER SEVEN

Never before—and God willing, may it never be so again—had there been an invasion armada the equal of the 1,600 seagoing ships carrying 545,000 American GIs and Marines that streamed across the Pacific in that fateful spring of 1945 bound for the island of Okinawa. In firepower, troops, and tonnage it eclipsed even the more-famous D day in Normandy on June 6, 1944. In that invasion, except for the enormous thirty-to-one preponderance in air power conferred upon him by 12,000 aircraft, General Eisenhower commanded only 150,000 Allied assault troops (compared to Lieutenant General Simon Bolivar Buckner's attacking force of 184,000 GIs and Marines). True, Eisenhower's supporting craft would eventually number 5,300, but most of these were far from being seaworthy. And the Allied naval forces off the five Normandy landing beaches could not approach the firepower of Admiral Spruance's Task Force Fifty-eight. Nor was there any comparison in the distances traveled from staging area to battleground. Only about 30 miles of English Channel separated southern England from western France, or at most perhaps 400 miles to faraway ports in the United Kingdom, but ships leaving the

West Coast ports of embarkation at San Francisco and Seattle
sailed 7,355 miles to the target. Yet, in feats of unrivaled seamanship still not generally recognized, the 1,300 ships arriving
off the Hagushi Beaches of Okinawa did get there in time for the
landings. And there were still 300 left behind in the various anchorages stretching across the western ocean.

From Seattle and San Francisco no fewer than 3,200 miles
had to be traversed before these newest and farthest-away vessels
could reach Hawaii, the point from which the stupendous American counter-attack was launched to its last battle 4,155 miles
distant. Soon these ships were putting in at the island battlegrounds whose names they bore (Guadalcanal, Bougainville, Tarawa, and the lesser battles of the Gilberts and Marshalls, New
Britain, the Admiralties, Buna, and Sidor) to begin the long drive
up the New Guinea coast—then staging up through the latest
battlegrounds at Peleliu, Leyte, and Saipan-Tinian-Guam. Under
the Stars and Stripes they roved boldly and unmenaced across
that Pacific Ocean that was now an American lake, for the Philippines were by then subdued; of the mighty Japanese Navy that
was to guard the Greater East Asia Co-Prosperity Sphere—Japan's euphemism for its stolen empire there—only great *Yamato*,
the most powerful warship afloat, had survived the holocaust of
disaster of the Battle of Leyte Gulf. Of the emperor's glorious
young eagles whose sneak attack on the Day of Infamy had awak-
ened the sleeping American giant, only a few weary veterans remained to join the ragged remnant of Japanese airpower. British
warships were also in the invasion fleet, a fast carrier force of
twenty-two vessels, for in Europe the gate had been found open
at Remagen Bridge, American troops were over the Rhine, and
the Old Queen of the Waves was sending help to her erstwhile
daughter, now Sovereign of the Seas.

Fleet Admiral Nimitz was still in overall command in Hawaii
as he had been when the Japanese were stopped at Midway, when
the long charge began at Guadalcanal. Admiral Raymond Spru-

ance commanded the Fifth Fleet, and there was the saltiest salt still giving orders to the expeditionary force. Vice Admiral Richmond Kelly Turner had brought the Marines to Guadalcanal and now, nearly three years later, still roaming his flagship bridge in an old bathrobe, still a profane perfectionist with beetling brow and abrasive tongue, a matchless planner who would also not scruple to tell the coxswain how to beach his boat, Kelly Turner was bringing the Tenth Army to Okinawa. Many of the officers and men aboard Turner's ships—especially the Marines—were not ecstatic to have the Old Salt in charge.

The Leathernecks could not forget his monstrous blunder at Guadalcanal, when he was the Amphibious Force commander at this first invasion in the long-awaited American counter-offensive. In the night of August 8–9, 1942, the Battle of Savo Island—better known to the sailors and Leathernecks involved as "the Battle of the Four Sitting Ducks"—Turner had lost four cruisers: *Astoria*, *Quincy*, *Vincennes*, and the Australian *Canberra*, while a fifth, *Chicago*, had its bow blown off. He lost them because he violated a commander's basic principle: never act on the premise of what you *think* the enemy will do but what he has the *capacity* to do. Thus, he was unprepared for battle when a Japanese task force led by Rear Admiral Gunichi Mikawa, the hero of Pearl Harbor, came tearing down the Slot the day after the Americans landed to surprise Turner in a disaster that might have been a catastrophe. Guadalcanal might have been reconquered by the enemy but for the tenacity of the Marines whom Turner quickly abandoned—and wisely so, his fire support force having been almost annihilated—sailing away with empty transports and some supply ships not even half unloaded, others still deep in the water. And the U.S. Navy did not return to Guadalcanal in force until three months later. But for Turner's friendship with Nimitz, he might have lost his head just as Admiral Husband Kimmel did at Pearl Harbor. But he did come back again and again—risking his ships in the submarine-infested waters of the Coral Sea, to bring reinforcements and badly needed supplies to Major General Alexander Vandegrift.

This writer well remembers the Four Sitting Ducks, for our battalion was lost in the jungle that night, and the monster explosions that shook the trees and flames that seemingly set the clouds on fire were not suggestive of good times to come. When we returned to the beach the next day and saw not a single ship on a bay that had been full of masts twenty-four hours earlier, we knew that we were all alone. Worse, our ship, the *George F. Elliott*—an African slaver if ever there was one—had been sunk on D day by a Zero that crashed her amidships, sending all our supplies—beans, bullets, and barbed wire—down to the bottom, along with our extra clothing and mosquito nets, so that many of us quickly came down with malaria, and the first time I shot a Jap, I had Jap clothing on. We also lived on wormy Japanese rice for the next few months. Worse for me, the portable typewriter that my mother had given me on my sixteenth birthday also sank into Davy Jones's locker, thus wrecking my naïve plan to fight by day and write by night.

So those Americans sailing toward Okinawa who had been on "the Canal" were not enchanted to have Kelly Turner at the helm again. It was well known that he was a constant thorn in Vandegrift's flesh, trying to take personal command of the reinforcements he brought to the island, planning to deploy them in tactical traps when actually he had no authority on land and knew exactly nothing about ground warfare. One infuriated officer wrote: "Turner was a martinet; very, very gifted, but he was stubborn, opinionated, conceited . . . thought that he could do anything better than anybody in the world . . . By and large naval officers, they were wary of trying to run land operations, but Turner, no; because Turner knew everything!"

Soldiers who served at New Georgia in the Solomons also were given a sampling of Admiral Turner's hectoring style when he was playing general—especially Major General Oswald Griswold, commander of the Army Fourteenth Corps. Turner repeatedly usurped Griswold's authority, divided his staff, and—his critics maintained—prolonged what turned out to be a miserable campaign. Whether or not General Simon Bolivar Buckner was aware of Turner's tendency to interfere is not known, and it may be that the Tenth Army commander as a newcomer to the Central Pacific was unfamiliar with the amphibious chief's abrasive personality.

Buckner was the son of the Confederate general of the same name, so often described by many military historians as "famous." Actually, Buckner's father was rather more infamous throughout the Southland, for it was he who had accepted the humiliating terms of unconditional surrender of Fort Donelson offered to him by his fellow West Point cadet U. S. Grant. It was to Grant that this adjective *famous* really applied, for he *did* become famous— not only because his capture of Donelson was received in the North with delirium (these were the early dark days of defeat and retreat for the Union) but also because his initials *U.S.* fitted his feat, and he became known thereafter as "Unconditional Surrender" Grant. Buckner junior—for some inexplicable reason called "the Old Man of the Mountain"—was definitely unlikely to submit to the sort of bluff Grant ran on his father. A big man, ruddy-faced and white-haired, avid for the conditioning of troops, he had served four years in Alaska and the Aleutians, where he had improved the defenses of the North Pacific. He had hoped to lead the invasion of Japan from this region, but the thrust from the Aleutians was never made. Instead it was coming from the Central Pacific, and Buckner had been called to Hawaii to lead it. His command was the Tenth Army, a new number for seven old divisions. These were the Seventh, Twenty-seventh, Seventy-seventh, and Ninety-sixth Infantry Divisions of the U.S. Army Twenty-fourth Corps commanded by Major General John

Hodge, and the First, Second, and Sixth Marine Divisions of the Third Amphibious Corps under the silver-haired veteran of Guadalcanal, Major General Roy Geiger.

All of these troops, and especially the replacements who fleshed out formations left understrength by battle losses, disease, or accident, hated the Pacific with a fierce, personal venom. Upon arriving in the islands they stood breathless at the rail of their transports, drinking in the beauty of a tropical paradise seen from the sea, especially at sunrise or sunset. But then, when they went ashore—even on a peaceful island—they saw the backside of beauty, a face as hideous as Medusa's. The first to be so disillusioned by the ambivalent South Seas were the men of the First Marine Division when they came on deck the morning of August 7, 1942, who stood at the rail of their ships studying Guadalcanal. My buddies and I—waiting to follow our machine guns down the cargo nets to the wooden Higgins boats waiting and wallowing in the swells—were enchanted until after we landed. Years later, I remembered that scene:

> She was beautiful seen from the sea, this slender long island. Her towering central mountains ran down her spine in a graceful east-west keel. The sun seemed to kiss her timberline, and lay shimmering on open patches of tan grass dappling the green of her forests. Gentle waves washed her beaches white, raising a glitter of sun and water and scoured sand beneath fringing groves of coconut trees leaning languorously seaward with nodding, star-shaped heads.
>
> She was beautiful, but beneath her loveliness, within the necklace of sand and palm, under the coiffure of her sunkissed treetops with its tiara of jeweled birds, she was a mass of slops and stinks and pestilence; of scum-crested lagoons and vile swamps inhabited by giant crocodiles; a place of spiders as big as your fist and wasps as long as your finger, of lizards the length of your leg or as brief as your thumb;

of ants that bite like fire, of tree-leeches that fall, fasten and suck; of scorpions without the guts to kill themselves, of centipedes whose foul scurrying across human skin leaves a track of inflamed flesh, of snakes that slither and land crabs that scuttle—and of rats and bats and carrion birds and of a myriad of stinging insects. By day, black swarms of flies feed on open cuts and make them ulcerous. By night, mosquitoes come in clouds—bringing malaria, dengue or any one of a dozen filthy exotic fevers. Night or day, the rains come; and when it is the monsoon it comes in torrents, conferring a moist mushrooming life on all that tangled green of vine, fern, creeper and bush, dripping on eternally in the rain forest, nourishing kingly hardwoods so abundantly that they soar more than a hundred feet into the air, rotting them so thoroughly at their base that a rare wind—or perhaps only a man leaning against them—will bring them crashing down.

And Guadalcanal stank. She was sour with the odor of her own decay, her breath so hot and humid, so sullen and so still, that all those hundreds of thousands of Americans who came to her during the ensuing three years of war cursed and swore to feel the vitality oozing from them in a steady stream of enervating heat.

The same reaction was felt by Buckner's troops at the same island—then a huge staging area—and from the same division. Staff Sergeant George McMillan wrote of the Marine replacement on Guadalcanal who ran from his tent at dusk and began to pound his fists against a coconut tree. "I hate you, goddamit, I hate you," the man cried, sobbing, and from another tent came the cry: "Hit it once for me!"

Almost all the troops of Buckner's Tenth Army shared this loathing, for they had not enjoyed malaria or monsoons or playing hide-and-seek with crocodiles or scorpions, snakes or poisonous centipedes. Indeed, as late as February 1945, General Hodge's infantry divisions were still mopping up on Leyte in weather and terrain exactly duplicating Guadalcanal's. Hodge was dismayed. A veteran and respected infantry commander who had served during the mop-up at Guadalcanal under the famous "Lightning Joe" Collins—a future Army chief of staff—and had again defeated the Japanese on New Georgia and Bougainville in the Solomons, as well as Leyte, Hodge knew that his troops were dearly in need of what is today called "Rest and Rehabilitation": i.e., a rousing beer-and-girls furlough in Melbourne or Sydney, Australia; Wellington, New Zealand; or even Manila. But he was not able to withdraw them from combat until March 1, with D day at the Great Loo Choo scheduled for April 1—exactly a month away. Yet, like the Marines training on Guadalcanal, when the GIs heard that their next campaign was to be on Okinawa, they were inexplicably reassured—perhaps because that island's highest temperature of 85 degrees in no way approached the "paradise" reading of 120.

Before landing day, meanwhile, the Seventy-seventh Division would be in action on the Kerama Islands. GIs of the Seventy-seventh—known as "the Statue of Liberty Division" because of its shoulder patch—had fought at Guam alongside those fuzzy-cheeked Marine youngsters who pinned on them the nickname of "the old Bastards." Their commander was Major General Andrew Bruce, who had also led them on Leyte. They were the first in action because Admiral Turner, having already felt the shudder of a "*kamikazed*" ship beneath his feet, wanted a safe group of islands with deep anchorages to be used as a "ships' hospital" to which the victims of Japanese suiciders could be towed and repaired. General Hodge also wanted a base for long-range artillery to support his corps's landing.

On the night of March 25, the Marines of Major Jim Jones's veteran Reconnaissance Battalion paddled their rubber boats to Kerama to scout the enemy. Reassured by their reports of little opposition, the Seventy-seventh landed there the next day, destroying the lairs of Ushijima's suicide boats as they took the reef islets one after another.

On the morning of March 29, soldiers of the 306th Infantry* realized how cruel their enemy could be. In a valley below their position they found about 150 dead and wounded Okinawan civilians, many women and children among them. They had disemboweled themselves with grenades the Japanese had given them, after telling them the Americans would torture and murder the men and rape the women. In another three days Hodge's two other divisions would be storming those Hagushi Beaches that Ushijima had chosen not to defend.

Major General James Bradley's Ninety-sixth Division would be on the right flank of the Twenty-fourth Corps assault. Fresh from Leyte's jungle and depleted by losses suffered during the fierce battle for Catmon Hill (and like Hodge's other divisions denied replacements meant for them but sent to Europe to help crush Hitler's last gasp in the Battle of the Bulge), the Ninety-sixth would face a far more punishing ordeal of blood and mud while attacking Ushijima's monster Swiss cheese of steel and rock. The soldiers of the Ninety-sixth called themselves "the Deadeyes" because Brigadier General Claudius Easley, the division's assistant commander, was a crack shot, a somewhat illogical extension of the part for the whole; especially in a formation so recently formed and new to combat.† In the division's spearheads would be the 381st Regiment, under Colonel Michael "Screamin'

---

* This means "regiment," not division. In American military parlance a regiment formed by three battalions is known by its "arm." Thus the First Regiment of the First Marine Division is called "First Marines," or the Seventh Regiment of the First Cavalry Division "Seventh Cavalry." Too often historians with no military experience mistake these designations to mean division, a much larger formation that—whether infantry, cavalry, or Marine—is usually formed by three "line" regiments and an artillery regiment with other special troops.

† This comment in no way is intended to demean these gallant GIs—or anyone who has looked upon the horrid Medusa face of battle—but appears only because it might be asked why other nicknames are mentioned but not the Ninety-sixth's.

Mike" Halloran, and Colonel Edwin May's 383rd. Eddy May was
a fine commander whose iron discipline was softened by his compassion for his troops. General Hodge considered him the finest
soldier in the entire Twenty-fourth Corps.

On the left flank of Hodge's zone would be his most experienced division: the Seventh, called "the Hour-Glass Division"
because of its shoulder patch and commanded by Major General
Archibald Arnold. Its GIs had seen action at Attu in the Aleutians
with their subzero cold, then Kwajalein in the Marshalls with its
decidedly yet infinitely more amenable heat, and finally those
dripping, enervating, malarial jungles of Leyte. In corps reserve
would be the 382nd Regiment of the Ninety-sixth Division, while
the Seventy-seventh Division still engaged in mopping up the
Keramas would be committed to the down-island attack once the
landings at Hagushi had been completed, Yontan and Kadena
Airfields had been seized, and the Twenty-fourth Corps wheeled
right (or south) to attack Ushijima's Swiss cheese.

Probably the most experienced and famous formation in the
American armed forces was the First Marine Division of Major
General Geiger's Third Amphibious Corps. On Guadalcanal
alone—where on August 7, 1942, its Leathernecks landed to
launch the long, three-year American counter-offensive—they
had been in combat a total of 142 days (from the landing date
until December 26), probably a record for sustained combat without relief, if such statistics are kept anywhere. During this five-
month campaign, which turned the tide of the Pacific War against
Japan, these men of "the Old Breed" were responsible for destroying most of the fifty thousand Japanese who fell on "Death
Island." In this dreadful carnage they were assisted by General
Collins's infantry after command passed to the Army on December 9, 1942, and especially by General Geiger's "Cactus" Air
Force, the Marine, Navy, and U.S. Army Air Force pilots who
literally blasted the once-dreaded Japanese Zero fighter out of the
South Pacific skies while littering the bottom of its waters with

sunken Nipponese ships. After "the island," the First fought in the vicinity of Finschhafen, captured Cape Gloucester on New Britain, and seized Peleliu at a cost of 1,749 dead and wounded while exterminating its 4,000 Japanese defenders. Major General Pedro del Valle commanded the First. Born in Puerto Rico, he had been graduated from Annapolis, serving as an observer in Ethiopia with Italy's Marshal Pietro Badoglio. Becoming an artillery expert, his guns had much to do with the victory at Guadalcanal.

The Sixth Marine Division was commanded by another Guadalcanal veteran: Major General Lemuel Shepherd, who would one day be commandant of the U.S. Marine Corps. His was an unblooded unit, sometimes called "the New Breed," yet 70 percent of its men and officers were veterans of combat in orphan regiments that had been combined under the Sixth's emblem of the silver Crusader's Sword. Only two of its twelve rifle battalions had never known "the music" of bombs and bullets, and among its battle-wise veterans were Lieutenant Colonel Victor Kulak, a belligerent bantam called "the Brute," the sarcastic nickname that Annapolis midshipmen pinned on all the coxswains of its rowing crews. In the ranks of this most gung ho of Marine divisions were such improbable swashbucklers as twenty-year-old Corporal Donald "Rusty" Golar, the self-styled Glory Kid. A brawny redhead, Rusty had fought with the Twenty-second Regiment on Guam and won a Bronze Star. "I'm a storybook Marine," he would say, grinning when his buddies laughed outright. "I'm lookin' for glory, and I'm lookin' for Japs." There were glory boys from collegiate football, too. Colonel Alan Shapley, commander of the Fourth Marines, had been one of the Naval Academy's finest athletes. Lieutenant George Murphy of the Twenty-ninth Marines had been captain of the Notre Dame football team.

In General Geiger's Third Corps reserve was the Second Marine Division. Its Second Marines had joined the original landing on Guadalcanal to be joined later by their comrades of the entire division. Derisively nicknamed "the Hollywood Marines" because they were based in California, they were not playacting when they waded ashore at Tarawa in 1943 to take in four days the island citadel that Rear Admiral Keiji Shibasaki had claimed could not be captured by "a million men in ten thousand years." They went on to fight the grinding battle at Saipan in 1944. Major General Thomas Watson still commanded the Second. Because his Leathernecks had staged the eminently successful feint of the textbook shore-to-shore operation at Tinian, he had been asked to do it again at the Minatoga Beaches on Okinawa.

It was fitting that the commander of the Third Amphibious Corps, which included these three Marine divisions, should be Geiger, the gruff and grizzled white bear of a man more prone to deeds than words. Though a flying general, he had been in so many other invasions since Guadalcanal and had devoured so many textbooks on tactics that he had emerged as an excellent leader of ground troops as well.

Finally, Tenth Army's Seventh Division—the Twenty-seventh Infantry commanded by Major General George Griner—was to be in "floating reserve" at Okinawa. If all went well there, the Twenty-seventh would occupy the island as a garrison division. For a division supposedly blooded in combat, such an assignment was not particularly dangerous, but the Twenty-seventh's record in the Pacific had not been outstanding. A New York National Guard outfit, the Twenty-seventh saw its first action on Makin, where sixty-five hundred of its GIs landed on November 20, 1944. On the first night many of these half-trained guardsmen were panicked by Japanese scare tactics. Actually, the enemy numbered only five hundred lightly armed garrison soldiers holding paper-thin fortifications. But they held out for a week, though outnumbered thirteen to one and with almost no artillery to match the overwhelming American superiority in ordnance. Dur-

ing this delay the escort carrier *Liscome Bay* was sunk on the last
day of battle, with a large loss of life. It was not the fault of the
troops—it never is—for as Napoléon said: "There are no bad
regiments, only bad colonels."

Many of the Twenty-seventh's officers from Major General
Ralph Smith down to the lowliest second lieutenant were ineffective; in fact, they were so indifferent to their responsibility that
during maneuvers in Hawaii more than a few of them checked
into Honolulu hotels for a night of revelry while their men slept
on the bare ground. Again on Saipan under Smith the Twenty-
seventh in between two Marine divisions moved so slowly that it
lagged fifteen hundred yards behind these advancing formations.
Thus a giant U was formed with the Twenty-seventh at the base,
presenting the enemy with an unrivaled opportunity to exploit it.
Immediately Marine Lieutenant General Holland M. "Howlin'
Mad" Smith, commander of the Fifth Corps, relieved Ralph
Smith and replaced him with another Army general. This episode
exploded with the loudest bang of the Pacific's shameful Army-
Navy rivalry. Prior to Saipan five Army generals had been relieved
in the Pacific, but that had been by *Army* generals. For a *Marine*
general to have the insolence to remove an *Army* general was to
join cardinal sin to unforgivable insult. Actually, the Twenty-
seventh improved after General Griner took command, and he
was still in command at Okinawa, with many brave men eager to
follow him and redeem their division's honor—which they would
do. The Twenty-seventh was not at full strength, only 16,143
men, compared to the 22,000 of the other Army divisions and the
24,000 for the Marines—which brought their replacements with
them.

Altogether, General Buckner's seven combat divisions numbered 183,000 men, of whom 154,000 would be in assault on the
Hagushi Beaches—half again as many as Ushijima's 110,000, although many of the Japanese commander's troops were raw Oki-

nawa conscripts. However, traditional military doctrine specifies
that an attacking force, especially an invader from the sea, should
possess at least a three-to-one superiority over the defense.

These, then, were the troops with which General Buckner
intended to make rapid conquest of Okinawa, unaware that only
at Peleliu had Americans encountered such a formidable fixed
position. At Okinawa Ushijima commanded at least twenty times
as many men and had fortified in depth ten times as many square
miles. That Buckner was unaware of the grueling, step-by-step,
shot-for-shot battle that awaited him was neither his nor his intelligence's fault, for the winter and spring clouds that shielded
the Great Loo Choo from the skies had made aerial pinpointing
of enemy defenses extremely difficult, while the Japanese, unrivaled at camouflage, had so artfully concealed their caves and cre-
vasses that a man might stand but a few paces from a 47 mm
antitank gun and never notice it.

Because Imperial General Headquarters wanted to bleed the
Americans white at Okinawa just as dearly as the United States
Chiefs of Staff desired to seize it, Ushijima was prepared to sac-
rifice every man in his command to soak the soil of the Great
Loo Choo in American blood.

In the wardrooms of the troop transports flowing up the curve of
the world, nervous planners pored over maps and those skimpy
aerial montages of enemy positions, some of them delighted that
there seemed to be so few pillboxes and blockhouses, others, more
practical—remembering Biak, Peleliu, and Iwo—scornfully ex-
claiming: "No resistance, huh? Wait till we get ashore!"

On the troop decks most of the conversation was about the
deadly habu, a long, thick, dark snake whose bite was supposed
to have no known remedy. Intelligence said the habu was something like a cobra, even displaying pictures of it. It was indeed a
venomous-looking reptile, but in the lighthearted way of the

American warrior, Buckner's troops made jokes about it, and the habu soon passed into the immortal GI-Marine menagerie of the goony-birds of Midway, the upside-down pissing-possum of Guadalcanal, Australia's lunatic-lunged kookaburra, the "beavers" of the North African beaches, the New Zealand kiwi, and the indecent snow-snake of Iceland. The men speculated so much about the habu that they almost forgot the Japanese, although officers frequently "held school" on the weather decks to stress the dangers of their objective.

"From Okinawa," one lieutenant told his platoon, "we can bomb the Japs anywhere—China, Japan, Formosa . . ."

"Yeah," a sergeant mumbled, "and vice versa."

It was true, of course, that the Japanese had sixty-five airfields on Formosa to the south and fifty-five on Kyushu to the north, as well as a few dozen scattered throughout the southern Ryukyus, but such discouraging information is not normally disseminated among the troops. More pointed and helpful information came from veterans such as Corporal Al Biscansin of the Sixth Marine Division, who offered this earnest advice to the boots:

"When you aren't moving up or firing, keep both ends down! The GI Bill of Rights don't mean a thing to a dead Marine."

The GI Bill rivaled the habu as a topic of conversation, for a surprising number of these young men intended to go to college when the war was over. They even expected that great event to happen soon.

"Home alive in '45," they said, a happy revision of Guadalcanal's gloomy estimate of "the Golden Gate in '48." They sang "Good-bye, Mama, I'm off to Okinawa," and joked about the latest horrendous estimates of American disaster broadcast by Radio Tokyo.

Admiral Ugaki had already made the mistake of believing that his airmen had crippled Spruance's fleet in those mid-March attacks and seriously delayed invasion of Okinawa. Because of his error, the Kerama Islands landings caught the Japanese unpre-

pared. Only Ushijima's handful of obsolete crates on Okinawa
and a few *kamikaze* from Kyushu were able to intervene, but they
inflicted only slight damage. Yet, on March 28, the GIs and Marines aboard the transports heard Radio Tokyo announce the
sinking of a battleship, six cruisers, seven destroyers, and one
minesweeper, and then the voice of an American-educated an-
nouncer simpering:

> This is the Zero Hour, boys. It is broadcast for all you Amer-
> ican fighting men in the Pacific, particularly those standing
> off the shores of Okinawa . . . because many of you will never
> hear another program . . . Here's a good number, "Going
> Home" . . . it's nice work if you can get it . . . You boys off
> Okinawa listen and enjoy it while you can, because when
> you're dead you're a long time dead . . . Let's have a little
> jukebox music for the boys and make it hot. . . . The boys
> are going to catch hell soon, and they might as well get used
> to the heat . . .

Then, having described the varieties of death instantly impending
for "the boys off Okinawa," the voice concluded: "Don't fail to
tune in again tomorrow night."

Two days later the voice was somber. "Ten American battleships, six cruisers, ten destroyers, and two transports have been
sunk. The American people did not want this war, but the au-
thorities told them it would take only a short while and would
result in a higher standard of living. But the life of the average
American citizen is becoming harder and harder and the war is
far from won . . ."

On March 31 the assault troops were given an eve-of-battle
feast. "We had a huge turkey dinner," the famous war correspondent Ernie Pyle reported. " 'Fattening us up for the kill,' the
boys said."

The next day Radio Tokyo had lost its audience: "The boys off Okinawa" had gone ashore.

That was on April 1—Easter Sunday, 1945, April Fool's Day, or L day, as it was called officially. The *L* stood for "Landing," but the Americans who hit the Hagushi Beaches with hardly a hand raised to oppose them had another name for it.

They called it Love Day.

Love Day

CHAPTER EIGHT

At 4:06 A.M. April 1, 1945, beneath still-darkened skies, Vice Admiral Richmond Kelly Turner aboard his flagship *El Dorado* gave the expeditionary force commander's traditional order: "Land the landing force!" Forty-five minutes later with the break of dawn the American bombardment force began firing that howling "typhoon of steel" that drove most terrified Okinawans into their storm caves and shook even those Japanese defenders—resolute moles that they were—deep inside their hollowed-out hills, caverns, concealed pillboxes, camouflaged blockhouses, and fortified lyre-shaped tombs.

Along eight miles of beaches ten battleships were firing, their huge turret guns ranging from twelve to sixteen inches in their bore diameter, hurling spinning shells weighing from twelve hundred to eighteen hundred pounds. Most of these battlewagons were obsolete, and some had been raised from the floor of Battleship Row at Pearl Harbor and been rebuilt. The ancient *Arkansas* had been commissioned well before World War I and had been ready for the scrap heap until Pearl Harbor Day kept her afloat. There they were: flagship *Tennessee, Colorado, Idaho, New*

Mexico, Texas, New York, West Virginia, Nevada, and, of course, *Arkansas.* Most of them shared a common defect: they were too slow to keep up with the modern fast carriers, and so had been refitted for shore bombardment. Normally, battleships fought other ships, firing armor-piercing shells on flat trajectories, but these off Okinawa had been adjusted to high-angle fire of high explosives strong and heavy enough to pierce and shatter enemy emplacements, and sometimes even to strike reverse slopes.

Interspersed in the gaps between the battlewagons, like the fingers of smaller hands fitted into those of bigger ones, were nine prewar heavy cruisers—veterans of every Pacific preinvasion bombardment. Joining them were three light cruisers and twenty-three destroyers, as well as dozens of those landing craft infantry (LCIs) that had been found too awkward for their designed mission of plowing up on enemy beaches and so converted to rocket fire. Americans boated in the amtracks following the rocket ships "in" cheered lustily when they heard that monster *swoooosh!* of those flights of missiles darkening the skies like so many arrows from thousands of bows.

Spruance's Fifth Fleet, besides the striking power of his TF 58 and the flying buffer of the British carrier force, also included ninety minesweepers of all types ready to clear Okinawan waters of the primitive contact mines planted by the enemy. There were also the brave SEALS, as they are now called, of the Navy's Underwater Demolition Teams, charged with detonating the enemy's underwater explosives and pointed stakes; the big bombers of the Twentieth Air Force, and the Tenth Army's own Tactical Air Force made up mostly of Marine pilots and commanded by a Marine, Major General Francis Mulcahy.

Here, off those eight miles of Hagushi Beaches, the heaviest weight of metal ever hurled from sea to shore was clearing the way for the assault troops—and yet, it was never needed. For all their thunder and flash, their geysering flame and smoke like so many erupting volcanos, the bombardment was falling harmlessly among beaches, hills, and valleys long ago abandoned by General Ushijima.

Even Ushijima and his staff standing atop Shuri Castle and studying the scene through binoculars were deeply impressed. One of these officers later wrote in his diary that the flash and crash of this incredible bombardment was "a scene of unsurpassed grandeur." They were also glad that Ushijima had accepted Yahara's advice not to defend the Hagushi Beaches. From what they saw they could imagine the carnage among their troops if he had adhered to the old, discredited doctrine of "destruction at the water's edge."

Yet for all its negligible effects, the titanic sea bombardment would serve one major psychological purpose: it would encourage the assault troops. Boated in their amphibious tractors—"amtracks"—in the bellies of their LSTs—"Landing Ship, Tanks," which they derisively called "Large Stationary Targets"—these men had been swallowing the smoke of their roaring vehicles for hours. Lined up on the tank deck two abreast, nose to rear, it was as though they were in a traffic jam, or sailing to battle in the Lincoln Tunnel. All—even the veterans—were tense and fearful, for they had been told that Okinawa would not be easy. Among some of the Marines it was more than anxiety that tied their stomachs in knots. They had breakfasted on "styke 'n' aiggs," a tradition they had picked up in Australia and New Zealand, and were having difficulty holding it down. Some ship's doctors hoped that they would all let it go over the side, once they were seaborne. "Steak and eggs!" one dismayed surgeon had cried. "A nice lot of guts that'll be to sew up—full of steak!"

Ernie Pyle smiled when he heard that complaint. Pyle had left the European Theater, in which the Axis had been driven to its knees, to travel with the Marines in the Pacific; and he was aboard one of those numerous LSTs when their big bow doors yawned open and the amtracks—roaring louder as the coxswains accelerated—began waddling down the tank decks to go plunging into the East China Sea. They could see ahead of them the white-capped gray water beneath a mackerel sky, and they could almost feel the impact of that monster howling seemingly encasing their heads in a great brass bowl on which some insane giant was hammering. Until that moment, the bombardment had been merely a steady rumbling noise outside. But now it was a bellowing, clanging clamor like Shakespeare's "iron tongue of midnight." None of these men of the assault troops were dismayed to hear this martial symphony overhead—big guns booming like kettledrums, shells speeding shoreward with the woodwinds' howl and the shriek of violins, the snare-drum rattle of machine guns together with a brass section of braying ack-ack, and beneath it all in counterpoint keeping the beat, the cough and hum of mortars like strummed cellos and bass viols. Rather, the GIs and Marines were delighted by the sound and the fury so suggestive of their enemy's destruction, and many of them grinned as they raised their helmeted heads above the gunwales or lifted their hands on high with the thumb and forefinger joined in the gesture of perfection.

Ernie Pyle, though exulting in his first experience of an amphibious invasion, was nonetheless a bit shaken by the bombardment, which he thought actually "set up vibrations in the air—a sort of flutter—which pained and pounded the ears as though with invisible drumsticks . . ." Even Kelly Turner—like all "Bomber Barons" or "Admirals of Artillery"—thought that the bombardment would end all opposition, reporting to Nimitz: "I may be crazy, but it looks like the Japanese have quit the war, at least in this sector." Back came the counter-message: "Delete all after 'crazy.' "

Nimitz would be proved a truer prophet, of course, but on Love Day Turner looked like a better bet. Off the beaches four thousand yards distant the control boats were organizing the attack waves. Perhaps eight hundred amtracks loaded with GIs and Marines were sent speeding beachward in from five to seven lines, each with bow waves curling away from their prows, their churning propellers leaving frothy white wakes trailing behind like tails a thousand yards long. Crawling steadily ahead of them were the amphibious tanks.

Abruptly, as though switched off, the beach bombardment ceased—and the GIs and Marines in the amtracks glanced skyward nervously, wonderingly. Actually the sea cannonade had been lifted only to strike enemy installations farther inland, and during the respite two flights of sixty-four carrier planes apiece came roaring over the beaches to strafe them with machine-gun fire—making the men in the amtracks lift their hands in approval once again. Usually the strafing planes raised only dust, but sometimes a Japanese fuel storage tank would be hit, and plumes of flame and clouds of smoke swirled skyward to enter drifting white clouds and suffuse them pink and black. Once the aircraft departed, the bombardment ships resumed their cannonade: this time firing every gun they mounted, even 40 mm AA spitting out red tracers flashing low across the water to explode just inland of the beach. Even so, all this also had not been needed—but woe to the commander who would have ordered anything else. Marines who had landed at Iwo Jima were still bitter over the less than adequate three-day preparation there, for when they came ashore they were instantly struck by hundreds of enemy positions that had been left intact. Three more days of steel and fire, they insisted, could not have failed to knock out all remaining obstacles on that tiny two-by-four island; and there would have been far fewer casualties than those twenty-two thousand dead and wounded United States Marines. That was why Okinawa got six days, with ships firing no less than seven thousand shells in every caliber from sixteen inches to 40 mm, plus the aerial onslaught. During the beach bombardment preceding H-Hour alone, the fleet fired 44,825 rounds of five- to sixteen-inch shells, 33,000 rockets, and 22,500 mortar shells. Seventy miles east of Okinawa Task Force Fifty-eight was deployed to furnish air support and to intercept air attacks from Kyushu, while support carriers were protecting troop carriers still arriving with second- and third-echelon troops. Earlier, carrier fighter-bombers had bathed the beaches in flaming tanks of napalm.

Thus, whether needed or not, this terrible weight of metal had made it certain that when the American spearheads climbed the reef to assault the beaches, not an enemy hand was raised to stop them.

Within the first hour no less than sixteen thousand troops had come ashore—an incredible achievement. With the beach-head secure, the remaining combat troops streamed onto Okinawa. They were followed by waves of tanks, some of them amphibious, some carried ashore by flotation devices, others ferried to the beaches by LSMs. Then came ammunition and supplies. Well before noon of April 1, 1945, the Hagushi Beaches were safely in American hands.

Down to the south off the Minatoga Beaches, meanwhile, the troops of Major General Watson's Second Marine Division also came roaring shoreward in a masterful feint that not only drew off some of Ushijima's defenders but actually—and unintentionally—brought upon their heads the wrath of the first *kamikaze* to strike the invaders. They damaged a transport and an LST, killing and wounding sixteen Americans. But the amtracks still churned beachward until, as the fourth wave crossed the line of departure at 8:30 A.M., with remarkable precision all the landing craft reversed course to return to their ships. Next day the demonstration was repeated, and General Ushijima reported that "an enemy landing attempt on the eastern coast of Okinawa on Sunday morning was completely foiled, with heavy losses to the enemy."

Inland on Hagushi the *Bimbo Butai* had broken and fled at the first belch of American guns, leaving the vital Yontan and

Kadena Airfields deserted and unprotected. By mid-morning the Sixth Marine Division on the left flank of General Buckner's four-division front had reached Yontan and was moving across it while the First Marine Division on its right struck out rapidly for Na-kagusuku Bay on the east coast, chopping up the remnants of the demoralized *Bimbo Butai*. Many of these reluctant soldiers, on both the Third Corps's front to the left and Twenty-fourth Corps's on the right, threw off the hated Japanese uniform and melted out of sight among their own people. Some true Japanese soldiers also shed their uniforms, not to desert but to don blue Okinawan kimonos to conduct guerrilla warfare from the wild northern hills. So there were few enemy indeed to contest the cross-island rush of the Tenth Army spearheads. Behind the ri-flemen, tanks had already rolled across beaches blessedly free of mines, while behind them came the bulldozers to cut passage through the terraces. Soon every manner of transport vehicle—wheeled or tracked—was depositing supplies on those rapidly growing inland mountains of cases, crates, and barrels. Every-where the engineers and pioneers of all the assault divisions were moving and shaking and transforming Okinawa with customary Yankee energy and ingenuity. Only the Battalion Aid Stations so rapidly organized on the beaches were quiet and inactive. Bottles of blood plasma or whole blood swung upside down and unused on their tall fork-like stands, while doctors and medics squatted on their heels or sat perched on water cans, smoking and staring wonderingly at empty operating tables like so many embarrassed supernumeraries.

Up front the attacking Americans were slowly letting out their breath. A soldier of the Seventh Division standing on a hill south of the Bishi River spoke for all of them when he said: "I've already lived longer than I thought I would." On his left the Marines were also submitting to the Great Loo Choo's pastoral charm, one of them feeding a box of K rations to a goat, which quickly gulped it down—cardboard and all—while others rounded up the shaggy little Okinawan ponies and vaulted aboard with shouts of glee.

"Ya-hoo!" one of them yelled. "I'm Captain Jinks of the Horse Marines!"

Out among the forest of masts in the Hagushi Anchorage Colonel Cecil Nist, General Hodge's intelligence officer, could hardly believe the radio reports from the beaches. The troops had found what the aerial photographs suggested: formidable but empty enemy positions, and now the suspicion that had replaced apprehension was gone, to be supplanted by relief. Major General Shepherd moved his Sixth Marine Division headquarters ashore with the remark: "There was a lot of glory on Iwo, but I'll take it this way."

Shepherd and his staff sailed past the new LST-hospitals riding lonely and unattended at anchor, with not even a single enemy aircraft threatening to plant the customary bomb in the center of that big red cross. On one of them assigned to the First Marine Division, the ship's surgeon was impatient. From the moment the amtracks rolled into the sea, his medical corpsmen had been at work transforming a ship-of-war into one of mercy. Litter left behind by the Marines was heaved over the side, the tank deck was hosed down and rows of cots set up inside it. Up forward the bow doors remained open and outside them a company of Seabees rigged a pontoon-pier for casualty boats. All was accomplished within two hours, and the ship's surgeon—a small, thorough, fussy man, obviously a perfectionist—strode out onto the pier, satisfied. He stood there, watching the columns of attacking Marines vanishing behind the seawall. But there was no bloody return traffic. Puzzled, he turned anxiously to a corpsman.

"No boats, no wounded?"

"Nothing yet, sir."

The surgeon shrugged, almost ruefully, and went back inside his LST. In a moment he had hastened outside again, having heard the sound of a boat's engine. A Marine was clambering out of it onto the pier.

"What's wrong with you, son?"

The Marine held up a hand spouting blood from one of his fingers.

"One of my buddies let one go and shot the top of my finger off."

The surgeon peered at it, turning to a corpsman to order it dressed.

"What's happening in there, son?"

"Don't ask me, Doc. All I know is everybody's goin' in standin' up."

The surgeon sighed. He glanced shoreward again, turning to go inside for lunch. Coming back to the pier, he still saw no return traffic. Calling to his solitary patient, he said: "C'mon, son, let's go make you a new finger. We've got plenty of time to do it in."*

That was Love Day on Okinawa, a most fortuitous eight hours of daylight during which the Tenth Army captured two airfields and a beachhead eight miles wide and three to four miles deep—all at a cost of 28 killed, 27 missing, and 104 wounded. Many of these were among the ranks of the Second Marine Division, supposedly having drawn the "soft" assignment of feinting

---

* This incident, reported by George McMillan in *The Old Breed*, his history of the First Marine Division in World War II, does not ring true. Marines are trained to keep their weapons on safety lock even during an invasion, and not to unlock them until a firefight is about to erupt or until receipt of enemy fire. "Let one go" is also untypical. "Got his gun off" is the proper slang. I can remember a corporal I learned to despise from Guadalcanal onward running toward the beach at Peleliu with terror on his face and holding his right hand aloft with the trigger finger missing and spouting carmine. My only comfort watching him sprint for the safety of the Battalion Aid Station on the beach was that his missing member would always remind him of his cowardice. So I doubt this episode—from the pen of a headquarters sergeant—and mention it only to show how absolutely unopposed the Okinawa invasion actually was at its beginning.

at the Minatoga Beaches. Down there another suicider put three holes in destroyer *Hinsdale,* and the stricken ship had to be towed to Kerama by tugs, the first invasion ship to achieve that dubious distinction. The next day when the Second's Marines made another demonstration, returning to their ships as planned, General Ushijima fired off an exultant report to Imperial General Headquarters claiming to have forced the enemy to withdraw "after being mowed down one after another."

Rather a different situation actually existed on Okinawa, where some fifty thousand Americans had come ashore almost unimpeded within a single day. Objectives expected to require three or more days and take many lives were firmly in American hands by nightfall. At Yontan Airfield there were bulldozers clearing away wrecked enemy planes and General Ushijima's clever dummies of sticks, stones, and cloth. Already there was an airplane approaching a runway. But it had a big red ball on its fuselage. Its roar as it circled became louder as bulldozers fell silent and Marines hopped to the ground clutching rifles. Others heating their rations with gunpowder fires stood erect and seized theirs, walking quietly toward the landing strip. The Zero swung seaward for a smooth landing.

The pilot wriggled out of his parachute pack. He climbed down to the tarmac. He walked toward the waiting Marines. He stopped. Between that moment in which he reached for his pistol, and the next when he slumped to the runway, riddled, an expression of indescribable horror had passed over his face.

"There's always someone," a Marine said ruefully—"there's always one poor bastard who doesn't get the word."

The Marines Overrun
the North

CHAPTER NINE

On the morning of April 2 American fighting men awoke in amazement to see vapor puffs issuing from their lips, their feet so chilled that they began to stamp them vigorously. The temperature was somewhere around fifty degrees and would not go above sixty, and most of these men with their blood thinned by years in the tropics felt as though they had arisen on the Arctic Circle. Actually, they welcomed a respite from the tropic heat with all its poisonous reptiles and vegetation and diseases, and they were again surprised to draw new issues of wool and gabardine field jackets to warm them—a tribute to the service of supply if there ever was one.

They moved out rapidly along the narrow roads—the GIs heading south, the Marines marching east and north—passing through peaceful fields plotted and pieced around little thatched farm cabins, each sheltered behind stone walls or bamboo windbreaks. Leathernecks of the Sixth Division—who now proudly called themselves "the Striking Sixth"—quickly gathered momentum in their approach march to Colonel Udo's three thousand holding the mountain fastness. Their first objective was

Zampa Cape to give Admiral Turner the site for a badly needed
radar station to warn of approaching Japanese aircraft, while the
First struck east across-island for Nakagusuku Bay, believed to be
an excellent anchorage and soon to be called Buckner Bay.

"Off and on!" the sergeants shouted as the men finished their
morning rations. "Get a move on, you mother's mistakes—an'
keep both ends up!"

"You there, Drag-Ass, whattaya lookin' behind you for?"

"I can't help it, Sarge—I keep feelin' somebody's gonna cold-
conk me from behind."

"Oh, yeah? Well, if anybody does—it'll be me!"

This mood of incredulity at the ease of the landing was a
common sensation among the Americans as Love Day turned into
Honeymoon Week on Okinawa. It was even more pronounced
in the north, where only Colonel Udo and his men stood between
the Marine divisions and their objectives. For the First, with its
memories of fierce battle, the Great Loo Choo was an unbeliev-
able but lovely frolic. In the afternoon General Del Valle called
a press conference to tell the correspondents: "I don't know
where the Japs are, and I can't offer you any good reason why
they let us come ashore so easily. We're pushing on across the
island as fast as we can move the men and equipment." They
were, and in two days of "fighting" the First's casualties totaled
three dead and eighteen wounded. On April 3 the division's ju-
bilant Marines stood on the eastern seawall overlooking the bay
and the Pacific Ocean. That same day scouting parties entered
the narrow finger of the Katchin Peninsula, traversing it without
opposition. Encouraged, General Buckner lifted all restrictions on
the rampaging First, and the division rapidly secured all the east
coast between Yontan Airfield and the Ishikawa Isthmus, that narrow neck of land about two miles wide lying two-fifths of the way
up Okinawa's slender length. In four days, the First had taken
territory expected to require three weeks of savage fighting.

To the north, the Sixth was running into steadily stiffening

opposition, ambushes, and isolated attacks on strong-points—
skirmishes real enough to those who fought in them, especially
those who died or fell wounded—but not in sufficient strength
to slow the Sixth's rapid advance. After the division had sealed
off the northern side of Ishikawa, its men started marching north
for Zampa Cape at route-step speed. The First would clean up
behind the Sixth, and also attend to the problem of the Okinawan
refugees now clogging the roads.

There were so many of them: women with babies at their
breasts; children without parents; grizzle-bearded ancients hob-
bling along with bent backs, leaning on staffs and carrying pitiful
small bundles representing all that the war had left them, that
terrible war that had also robbed them of the authority of their
beards and had exposed them to Japanese mockery and American
pity; and the old white-haired women who could not walk, who
merely squatted in the road, shriveled, frail, hardly bigger than
monkeys, waiting to be carried, waiting for the kind Marine who
might stop and stick a lighted cigarette between their toothless
gums.

They were a docile people, and now they were terrified because the Japanese had told them the Americans would torture
them. They were frightened also because they knew that among
them were Japanese soldiers disguised as civilians. But their fear
vanished with gentle treatment, with the policy of carefully
searching all males between fifteen and forty-five—to discover
many a knife or cartridge belt beneath a smock—and of placing
all of these within prisoner-of-war camps. Soon the Okinawans
were speaking openly of their hatred for the Japanese, their loathing for the Reign of Radiant Peace.

"Nippon ga maketa," they said. "Japan is finished."

Marines of the Sixth Division were still marching rapidly
north, sweeping up both coasts, a regiment to either side, and
making giant strides daily. Tanks packed with grinning riflemen

rolled up the narrow, dusty roads unimpeded but for an occasional sniper, a hastily built and unforbidding roadblock that bulldozers or the tanks themselves could easily shove aside, or here
and there an obviously freshly planted land mine that could be
detonated with a well-aimed rifle shot.

On April 8 the tanks in the lead came to the mouth of the
Motobu Peninsula, a wild headland jutting into the East China
Sea on the left, or west of the Marines. Here the Americans discovered why it was that they had moved so easily north. On
Motobu were gathered almost all of the two thousand soldiers
remaining to Colonel Udo. They were holed up on twelve-
hundred-foot Mount Yaetake, among the well-chosen and well-
fortified labyrinth of cave-eaten ridges, cliffs, gorges, steep hills,
and rocky corridors—well supplied with guns, prepared to fight
to the end.

The Marines moved in. They pushed cautiously around the
coastal roads, their engineers swiftly building bridges over the
ruins of those demolished by the Japanese or trucking in loads of
rock and dirt to fill tank-traps blasted at the foot of cliffs or out
in the rice paddies. By April 13 they had driven the Japanese back
onto the crest of the Yaetake stronghold. They were prepared to
attack in a pincers, three battalions to begin a fighting climb from
Motobu's west coast, two to strike from the east.

With first light on Friday the thirteenth on Okinawa, these
Marines of the Sixth Division were startled, then grief-stricken,
to hear the bullhorns of the ships offshore blaring:

"Attention! Attention! All hands! President Roosevelt is dead.
Repeat, our supreme commander, President Roosevelt, is dead."

Swiftly the news reached the men out of earshot. Many of
them cried, most of them prayed. So many of these youths had
known no president other than Franklin Delano Roosevelt. They
had truly loved him, had depended on him—how much they did
not know until they heard that he was dead. Nor could they turn

for solace to company officers, barely a few years their senior. They could ask only: "What do we do now?"

Memorial services might be possible on ships even now flying the flag at half-mast, but the Marines on Motobu could do nothing but move out.

The Yaetake attacks became a week-long nightmare against a phantom enemy. Everywhere in the hills were small groups of Japanese clustering around a Hotchkiss heavy machine gun and the usual proliferation of Nambu lights. Marines might grenade these nasty spitting nests, might call down exact mortar fire, but then, in the succeeding rush, might find nothing but a trail of blood to suggest that anyone had struck at them.

"Jeez!" a Marine swore. "They've all got Nambus, but where the hell are they?"

On April 15 naval gunfire and close-up air strikes grew stronger. More artillery was brought in. Artillery observers went forward, among them a battery commander and his spotter, Pfc. Harold Gonsalves. The commander lived because Gonsalves hurled himself on a Japanese grenade to save him—and win the Medal of Honor.* More and more guns lashed at Yaetake.

Next day the Marines drove deeper into the Japanese complex. Corporal Richard Bush led a squad forward on the right flank of the three-battalion line, striking at Yaetake's eastern mass. The face of the opposing ridge erupted with gunfire. Bush's squad went up and over it to drive the Japanese out, to score the first breakthrough. But Bush was badly wounded. He was pulled back

---

* Here is perhaps the most moving of all the phenomena of the war: the self-sacrifice of noble and brave young American fighting men who smothered enemy grenades with their bodies to save their buddies. Yet, discussing this once with a group of teachers, I had just begun to quote Jesus Christ's dictum "Greater love than this no man hath, that a man lay down his life for his friends," when one of them angrily interrupted me. "Nonsense!" he cried in scorn. "Who would do such a crazy thing?" Glaring at me, he asked with heavy sarcasm, "Would you?" I replied, "I might. But never to save someone like you."

to a cluster of protecting rocks where other men lay. A grenade sailed in. Bush pulled it to him. He saved the other wounded and he also lived, to join that amazing company of Marines whose Medals of Honor testified to the toughness of their bodies. Through the hole his squad had cut, through other holes along the line, the fight marched upward—swirling up in the mountains where it became as much a matter of supply as killing the enemy.

Marines toiled up hills with five-gallon cans of water on their backs and bandoleers of rifle-clips or grenades slung crisscross about their bodies. Battalion commanders going up to inspect the lines brought a water can or a mortar shell along with them.

It was four days before the Marines burst into Colonel Udo's headquarters to discover this mimeographed sheet intended for their eyes:

NEWS OF NEWS
No. 1
Saturday, April 14
President Roosevelt Died A Sudden Death
To the men of the Sixth Marine Division!

We take it a great honor to speak to you for the first time.

We are awfully sorry to learn from the U.P. telegraph that the life of President Roosevelt has suddenly come to its end at 3:30 P.M. on April 12. It seems to be an incredible story in spite of its actual evidence.

Men of the 6th Marine Division, particularly men of the 15th and 29th Marines and the 3rd Amphibious Corps, we express our hearty regret with you all over the death of the late President. What do you think was the true cause of the late President's death? A miserable defeat experienced by the U.S. forces in the sea around the island of Okinawa! Were this not the direct cause leading him to death, we could be quite relieved.

The American flag is raised over the First Marine Division cemetery on Okinawa, after the last battle of World War II, a battle of savage proportions.

ABOVE: Navy carrier planes soften up Japanese installations before the invasion.

RIGHT: Flights of missiles from the rocket ships opposite the enemy beaches go screaming toward the enemy.

Not even the D-day force in Normandy rivaled the huge invasion fleet gathered for Okinawa. Here in just one of the staging areas for the assault, supplies and ships are massed.

Some bewildered Okinawan refugees aboard a Navy amtrack on their way to a safe haven.

ABOVE: Unopposed because the Japanese commander of the defending Thirty-second Army wisely decided not to expose his troops to the dreadful American sea and air bombardment, Marines and GIs of the assault force were so relieved, as they moved inland, that they called Landing Day "Love Day."

RIGHT: Soon, U.S. troops suffer casualties. A wounded Marine is borne from the battlefield under heavy enemy pressure.

The body of a Japanese soldier killed by U.S. Tenth Army forces lies in front of an advancing tank.

While frontline troops consolidate their gains in mid-April 1945, these reserve soldiers of the Twenty-seventh Infantry Division—many of them weeping—kneel in prayer at a memorial service for their Commander in Chief, Franklin Delano Roosevelt, who died on April 12.

Dummy aircraft such as this one, made of bamboo (ABOVE), were intended to draw off American fire—which they did—but other, true planes, like this wrecked Zero fighter inside a revetment (BELOW), were destroyed from the air on the first day of the landing.

A flamethrowing tank of the Sixth Marine Division lays down a stream of fire on an Okinawan hillside in bitter fighting. Japanese soldiers fought fiercely, shielded in deeply protected caves from the American onslaught.

Navy Medical Corpsmen were among the bravest heroes
of Okinawa. Here they comfort a wounded Marine where
he fell, sending lifesaving blood plasma into his veins
from bottles hung on bayoneted rifles thrust into
the ground.

We do not think that the majority of you have exact knowledge of the present operations being carried out by the U.S. forces although a very few member of you must have got a glympse of the accurate situation.

An exceedingly great number of picked aircrafts carriers, battleships, cruisers and destroyers held on her course to and near the sea of Okinawa in order to protect you and carry out operations in concert with you. The 90% of them have already been sunk and destroyed by Japanese Special Fighting Bodies, sea and air. In this way a grand "U.S. Sea Bottom Fleet" numbering 500 has been brought into existence around this little island.

Once you have seen a "Lizard" twitching about with its tail cut off, we suppose this state of lizard is likened to you. Even a drop of blood can be never expected from its own heart. As a result an apopletic stroke comes to attack.

It is a sort of vice however to presure upon others unhappiness. This is why we want to write nothing further.

It is time now for you, sagacious and pradent, however, to look over the whole situations of the present war and try to catch a chance for reflection!!

The Marines went on to conquer the rest of Motobu, securing the peninsula on April 20. Above them, the Sixth Division's Twenty-second Regiment had reached Okinawa's northernmost point. The biggest battle in the northern sector was over.

The Sixth spent the rest of April patrolling and pursuing those Japanese who had fled Yaetake and turned irregular, using wardogs to scent the enemy and bark a warning. They even found that natural enemy of whom they had had such ample, ominous warning.

"Lookit the snake I just killed. It's one of them habu!"

"Hoo-what?"

"Habu, the snake they was all talkin' about before we landed."

"What're yuh gonna do with it?"

"Do with it! With the slop they been feeding us on this screwy island? I'm gonna cut it into fillets and then I'm gonna fry it and eat it!"

Marines of the First Division were not quite so desperate. They were, in fact, still celebrating the honeymoon, extending it for the duration of the month of April.

Many of the division's battalions built bivouacs complete with gravel paths, showers, and mess halls. The men went to abandoned Okinawan homes to remove the sliding panels that separated the rooms. They used them for foxhole covers or to build shanties. Everybody had a pet—a pony, a goat, even one of those numerous Okinawan rabbits that might have escaped the pot. There was an open-air theater at Division Headquarters, and there all the clerks and typists gathered nightly to play leapfrog until it was dark enough for a movie. This was not battle as the First had known it. But the men said, "Peace—it's wonderful!" They were so enchanted by "Lilac Time" that they brewed jungle juice out of their rations, drank it from "borrowed" lacquerware—one of Okinawa's few crafts—and began to harmonize.

They sang all the old favorites such as "The Wabash Cannonball" or "Birmingham Jail," as well as that vast repertoire of bawdies and unprintables collected or composed by local bards during three years of tramping the Pacific. There was a new printable one for Okinawa, and it went:

Oh, don't you worry, Mother, your son is safe out here.
No Japs on Okinawa, no sake, booze or beer.
Your sons can't find no Nips, so we're going back on ships.
But don't you worry, Mother, cause we're going on another.

But they were not. The honeymoon was ending. They were staying on Okinawa and going south, down to that Naha-Shuri-

Yonabaru line that had stopped the Army's Twenty-fourth Corps.

In the meantime, Admiral Ugaki had hurled the first of his *kikusui*—or "Floating Chrysanthemums"—aerial strikes on the American warships surrounding Okinawa; while Admiral Soemu Toyoda, Navy Chief of Staff, had also ordered great *Yamato*— the mightiest warship ever built—to join these *kamikaze* attacks as a suicide battleship.

"Floating Chrysanthemums"

CHAPTER TEN

In Japan the chrysanthemum is probably the most beloved of all flowers, woven into wreaths for weddings and funerals alike, decorating graves or dropped by grieving pilots onto waters in which their dearest comrades had plunged to their death. Thus, in conformance with this custom among the flower-loving Nipponese, Admiral Matome Ugaki decided to give the scheduled *Ten-Go* aerial attacks on American shipping the name of *kikusui*, or "Floating Chrysanthemums."

Although Ugaki's aerial strength on Kyushu had been seriously weakened by Halsey's strikes of mid-October 1944, and especially by Spruance's sweeps of March 18–19, 1945, he still had well over three thousand planes—both conventional and suiciders—in his command after the Americans landed on Okinawa.

Ugaki had few reservations about his ability to shatter the enemy fleet and so delay or even prevent the invasion of Japan proper, but he did occasionally despair about the absence of coordination and cooperation among the Army and Navy subordinate air commanders on both Formosa and Kyushu. Though the

Japanese command structure was probably better unified for Okinawa than for any other operation thus far, it was still a most
casual chain of command in which the last thing a subordinate
commander in, say, the Army, would think of doing was to obey
an order from a superior in the Navy. At best to them an order
was no better than a suggestion. Thus Army and Navy commanders on those two great island fortresses neither cooperated
with each other nor followed directives from the Combined Fleet
or Imperial Army Headquarters in Tokyo. Although there was
indeed intense and divisive rivalry between the American Army
and Navy in the Pacific, orders from superiors were never—or at
least seldom—ignored. If Fleet Admiral Nimitz issued orders to
Admiral Turner off Okinawa, he transmitted them to General
Buckner, who obeyed them without question.

Admiral Ugaki enjoyed no such luxury. If he wanted Lieutenant General Michio Sugahara, commander of the Sixth Air Army
on Kyushu, to take some action, he would not issue an order but
rather send a diplomatic officer to Sugahara's headquarters to ex-
plain in the least offensive language what was being required of
him. Such deference, of course, did not forge the Japanese chain
of command with iron links, and it also wasted valuable time, for
Ugaki was based at Kanoya and Sugahara at Chiran. Nor could
he ask Admiral Toyoda's fleet to issue an order binding on both
of them. All that Ugaki could do was to send orders to a pair of
Army air divisions that made most of the Okinawa attacks, although even here they were sometimes ignored. It is possible that
this deference by senior officers to their subordinates was the
result of Japanese misunderstanding of the character of Western
military officers. When Japan decided to build the Imperial Navy,
the model was the British Royal Navy, and the innate courtesy of
its officers was mistaken for reticence. Thus an admiral might
hesitate to insist that a commander give unbending obedience to
his orders lest it be considered rude.

Ugaki had a second problem in organizing his forthcoming

kikusui attacks: how to strike a balance between under-training and over-training his *kamikaze*. Overtraining a pilot in the sense of turning him into a skillful combat flyer would be a wasted effort when all that was needed was to guide an obsolete aircraft to its target and then crash-dive it. But suicide attacking wasn't that simple, especially in the North Pacific springtime when the weather was so variable, with conflicting wind currents, poor visibility, and low ceilings. In such weather even an experienced pilot could become lost. For a rookie pilot to keep a bomb-loaded crate on a direct course was not enough, for he still might not find his target. In such unreliable planes, engine trouble was frequent, and the student pilot needed to be trained enough to return successfully to base. But a new recruit would not emerge as a qualified suicider until months later. This requirement put an unbearable burden on Ugaki's attempt to build up a powerful air armada; the suicide tactic for which this force was being formed was not only innately self-destructive but also time-consuming. Japan in the spring of 1945 could not afford to lose more months of what had become a fast-vanishing resource. Finally, the American seaborne aerial attacks on Kyushu and Formosa, as well as the Mariana-based B-29 strikes on Kyushu and to a lesser degree of MacArthur's Fifth Air Force on Formosa, along with the willingness of the suicide-saviors to take their own lives, had left Ugaki with nothing like the minimal four thousand aircraft he needed to destroy or cripple Spruance's Fifth Fleet. That was one reason why Ugaki's airplanes did not immediately strike the Americans the day the invasion began, and it was not until that very day that Admiral Toyoda in Tokyo ordered *Kikusui* 1 to be launched on April 6.

That morning dawned overcast, with northeast winds whipping a mackerel sea into a white-crested gray mass, pushing layers of smutty clouds scudding along at altitudes of three thousand to seven thousand feet. It was good *kamikaze* weather, providing them with excellent cover. Yet Rear Admiral Toshiyuki Yokoi, whom Ugaki had placed in charge of the *kikusui* attacks, waited until around noon before sending his squadrons aloft, hoping thereby to catch patrolling American fighters at that most dangerous moment of refueling—either on carrier decks or the aprons of Yontan and Kadena Airfields. It was a good idea that may have come to Yokoi by his recollection of how Yamamoto's carriers at Midway were struck at exactly that moment. But there would be no such surprise, for Spruance's task force commanders had long since installed the routine of keeping defensive fighter patrols aloft from sunup till sundown. Nor did Yokoi's ruse of dropping "window"—aluminum strips to create false blips on radar screens to lure American fighters away from the impact area—for radar operators picked them up almost as soon as they were dropped.

Both Spruance and Turner were aware that a massive enemy aerial strike would arrive that day, not only from warnings from intelligence officers reading messages in the broken Japanese code, but through combat instincts sharpened by years of experience: once the enemy had collected enough planes, he would strike. To thwart him, Turner had deployed a wide circle of sixteen radar picket destroyers like irregular-length spokes in a wheel winding around Okinawa and some of its surrounding islands. These spokes extended from "Point Bolo," a reference point on that Zampa Cape he had so ardently desired, and which had been presented to him by the Sixth Marine Division. Each radar picket could give early warning of an enemy attack, and also carried a five-member radar direction team trained in vectoring patrolling fighters onto "bogies," unidentified targets. As might be expected, the pickets would become prime targets of the attacking enemy, especially Radar Picket Stations 1 through 4, on duty on an arc about thirty miles north of Okinawa—the point over which enemy planes from Kyushu were most likely to fly.

On that morning of April 6 all was quiet in the skies above

the Great Loo Choo, although Japanese scout planes in the northern Ryukyus had discovered TF 58's Fast Carrier Forces and brought hundreds of fighters and bombers down on them. Half of them missed their target and flew on to Okinawa while the other half zeroed in on Rear Admiral Joseph "Jocko" Clark's Task Group 58.1. They hit the carrier *Hancock* and two destroyers, and a *kamikaze* Judy bomber almost sent the big flattop *Bennington* to a watery grave. Plunging at the American's stern, the suicider was shot to bits by all of *Bennington*'s ack-ack that could be brought to bear. When the Judy exploded astern, parts of her engine fragments fell in a shower on the carrier, temporarily disabling her rudder.

Later in the day Yokoi's fighters arrived off Okinawa's airfields and were intercepted by American fighters on patrol above them. At three o'clock, with the Yankee fighters presumably driven from the area, the suiciders struck. They dove on the pickets of the radar screen and that forest of masts in Hagushi Anchorage. Some 200 of them came plummeting down for five hours until darkness veiled the sea or magnified the funeral pyres of stricken American ships.

Destroyers *Bush* and *Colhoun* were sunk, *Colhoun* hit and staggered so frequently that she had to be abandoned and sunk by friendly fire. The ammunition ships *Logan Victory* and *Hobbs Victory* also went down, creating a temporary ordnance shortage for the Tenth Army. Nine other destroyers were damaged, as were four destroyer-escorts and five mine vessels.

It was an impressive day's work for the first sally of the *kikusui* even though they had lost 135 planes. But the *kamikaze* reports were as usual exaggerated, rivaling even those of the Thirty-second Army, claiming thirty American ships sunk and twenty more burning. Such bloated estimates so encouraged Admirals Ugaki and Toyoda that the Navy chief began to think that perhaps the world's first suicide battleship—great *Yamato*—might really stagger the Americans during its one-way voyage to Okinawa and eternal glory.

Yamato—named for the clan generally credited with founding the Japanese nation—was not only the most powerful battleship afloat, but also the most beautiful. On April 6, while hundreds of *kamikaze* roared down from the north, *Yamato* came trailing afterward in the spreading white majesty of her mighty bow wave.

Yamato had survived the Battle of Leyte Gulf, where her sister *Musashi* had not. *Yamato* could outshoot anything in the U.S. Navy. She had nine 18.1-inch guns firing a projectile weighing 3,200 pounds a distance of 45,000 yards, compared to the 2,700-pound shell and 42,000-yard range of the American 16-inchers. She displaced 72,809 tons fully laden, and drew 35 feet. She was 863 feet long and 128 in the beam. She could hit 27.5 knots at top speed or cruise 7,200 miles at 16 knots. And she was sortying out of the Inland Sea for Okinawa with only enough fuel in her tanks for a one-way voyage.

If soldiers and tanks, fliers and airplanes, sailors and boats could be enrolled in the ranks of the suiciders, it was logical that admirals and dreadnoughts should follow. There were three admirals coming with *Yamato*, and the light cruiser *Yahagi* and eight destroyers. There might have been more of them and more warships, but Admiral Toyoda could scrape up only 2,500 tons of fuel for the venture. Although Toyoda had high hopes for the success of the *kikusui*, he could not have regarded *Yamato*'s sally as anything but a forlorn hope; he gave Rear Admiral Seichi Ito, commanding this Surface Special Attack Force, only two airplanes for protection. If it was the good fortune of *Yamato* and company to reach Okinawa unscathed, or at least with the huge battlewagon and a few other ships intact, their mission was to fall like wolves upon the sheep of the American troop transports and supply ships in the Hagushi Anchorage, and then, with their fuel almost exhausted, beach themselves to support a sally by Ushijima's Thirty-second Army with all their guns led by *Yamato*'s 18-inchers. At three-twenty on the afternoon of April 6, exactly twenty minutes after the first of the Floating Chrysanthemums dove on the Hagushi targets, *Yamato* and her escorts shoved off from Tokuyama.

There had been a ceremony. At six o'clock, all men and officers not on duty had been broken out on deck. A message from Admiral Jisaburu Ozawa, chief victim of the Americans' "Marianas Turkey Shoot," was read:

"Render this operation the turning point of the war."

The men sang the somber National Anthem, *"Umi Yukaba"*:

> *Across the sea, corpses in the water,*
> *Across the mountain, corpses in the field.*
> *I shall die for the Emperor.*
> *I shall never look back.*

Next the ship's company, convinced to the man that they would never survive this voyage, gave three Banzais for the emperor and returned to quarters. At ten o'clock, *Yamato* was in the Pacific Ocean—racing down Kyushu's eastern shores with her consorts gathering about her, shooing the American submarine *Hackleback* away, swinging to starboard off Kyushu's southern nose to sail west through Van Diemen Strait into the East China Sea.

Admiral Ito was taking the Surface Special Attack Force on a big swing west-northwest in hopes of pouncing on the Americans off Okinawa at about dusk of the next day.

But *Hackleback* had already alerted Admiral Spruance, and shortly before half-past eight the next morning a scout plane from *Essex* spotted the Japanese force just southwest of Kyushu, less than four hundred miles above Okinawa.

Patrol planes began taking off from Kerama-retto.

At ten o'clock, *Yamato*'s pathetic pair of fighter escorts flew back to Japan.

At ten-thirty Rear Admiral Morton Deyo was ordered to take six battleships, seven cruisers, and twenty-one destroyers north and place them between the approaching Japanese warships and the American transports. At almost the same moment the patrol planes found *Yamato* sailing at twenty-two knots in the middle of a diamond-shaped destroyer screen, with cruiser *Yahagi* trailing behind. The big planes shadowed the naked enemy fleet like vultures.

"Hope you will bring back a nice fish for breakfast," Admiral Turner signaled Admiral Deyo.

The commander of the intercepting force seized a signal blank and pencil to write his reply. "Many thanks, will try—" An orderly handed him an intercepted message. Scouts of the Fast Carrier Forces had found the enemy. Three groups totaling 380 planes were preparing to strike. "Will try to," Deyo concluded, "if the pelicans haven't caught them all!"

The "pelicans" had.

At half past twelve the American warbirds were over the target. Ten minutes later two bombs exploded near *Yamato*'s mainmast. Another four minutes and a torpedo had pierced her side. At the same moment destroyer *Hamakaze* stood on her nose and slid under, and *Yahagi* took a bomb and a fish and went dead in the water.

There was a respite.

The Americans came again at half-past one and planted five torpedoes in *Yamato*'s port side. Water rushed into boiler and engine rooms, and the stricken mammoth began to lean to port. Rear Admiral Kosaku Ariga, *Yamato*'s captain, ordered counterflooding in the starboard boiler and engine rooms. Ensign Mitsuru Yoshida attempted to warn the men there. Too late. They were sacrificed.

Still *Yamato* listed, and she had but one screw working. Her decks were a shambles of cracked and twisted steel plates. Her big guns would not work. The watertight wireless room was filled with water, and an explosion had wrecked the emergency dispensary and killed everyone inside.

At two o'clock the final attack began.

Hellcats and Avengers plunged from the skies to strike at the hapless ship. *Yamato* was shaken fore and aft and the entire battleship shuddered violently. Communications with the bridge were cut off, the distress flag was hoisted, the steering room became flooded, and with the rudder jammed hard left, mighty *Yamato* sagged over to a list of thirty-five degrees.

"Correction of list hopeless!" the executive officer cried.

Down came the Americans for the death blow.

"Hold on, men!" Ariga shouted. "Hold on, men!"

Bombs were striking around and upon *Yamato*, raising a giant clanging, flinging waves of roaring air across her decks, jumbling men together in heaps. Out of one pile crawled high-ranking staff officers. Admiral Ito struggled to his feet. His chief of staff arose and saluted him. The two men regarded each other solemnly. Ito turned, shook hands with each of his staff officers, wheeled, and strode into his cabin, either to embrace death or await it—the world will never know which. Admiral Ariga rushed to save the emperor's portrait, but met death instead.

Yamato was dying slowly, like the giant she was. Her decks were nearly vertical, her battle flag all but touched the waves, explosions racked her monster body, her own ammunition began blowing up—and all around her were her sister ships in death agonies. *Yahagi* was sinking, *Isokaze*, *Hamakaze*, *Asashimo*, and *Kasumo* had received their death blows.

At twenty-three minutes after two *Yamato* slid under, a full day's steaming from Okinawa.

Japan had lost her navy, the suicide battleship had failed, and it was now up to the *kikusui* and the men of Lieutenant General Mitsuru Ushijima.

Fiery Failure at
Kakazu Ridge

CHAPTER ELEVEN

The honeymoon had been brief for Major General John Hodge's Twenty-fourth Corps—hardly more than a weekend.

The day after Love Day, the Twenty-fourth's spearheads raced across the island, Seventh Division on the left, Ninety-sixth on the right, turning to their right (or south) the next day for the anticipated rapid down-island advance. Their progress seemed as bloodless as the Marine drive in the north.

But on April 4 they found resistance "stiffening."

It grew stiffer daily until, on April 8, "greatly increased resistance" was reported. They had come into the outerworks of Ushijima's Naha-Shuri-Yonabaru Line, and probably its most formidable position: Kakazu Ridge.

At first glance, Kakazu (pronounced "Cock-a-zoo") did not seem especially difficult: neither unusually high nor uncommonly steep. Three-quarters of a mile south the Urasoe-Mura Escarpment seemed a much more difficult natural barrier. That was what Colonel Eddy May thought when he prepared to send his 383rd Regiment of the Ninety-sixth Division against it. Studying Kakazu from his headquarters atop another ridge, he considered its seizure a preliminary to an assault on Urasoe-Mura. His maps suggested no other conclusion, although Colonel May was not aware that the map was probably made from photographs taken when the entire area was obscured by clouds. Kakazu was a rough coral hogback about a thousand yards long running from the coastal flats in the west on a northwest-southeast keel. It was formed by two hills of the smaller Kakazu West on May's right flank, and the larger Kakazu Ridge proper to his left.

What Colonel May—and General Hodges—also could not suspect was that Kakazu's defenders under Colonel Munetatsu Hara had been fortifying their position for months. Assisted by Okinawan laborers, they had constructed a subterranean honeycomb of caves, tunnels, and passageways. This would not be the first such "impregnable" position encountered by Americans in the Pacific War: what made it unique was its complete camouflage, its incredible variety and number of fortified positions, its depth, its abundance of supplies and ammunition—including a spigot-mortar unit launching huge 320 mm shells—its network of mutually supporting emplacements firing interlocking fire, and its absolute invulnerability to those nineteen-hundred-pound shells hurled at it by the battleship *Colorado* cruising offshore.

Because Colonel Hara had buried his headquarters deep below the main ridge, he had complicated his communications: his only problem. Although many tunnels had interconnecting passages and there were also voice tubes, some underground positions were isolated, compelling Hara to use runners who would be exposed to enemy fire once they appeared above ground. Hara had no fear of the Americans' plentiful and powerful tanks, so superior to the Japanese diminutive "kitchen sinks" that had been nevertheless unstoppable against inferior or lightly armed troops in the Manchuria-Burma-Philippines campaigns. Fronting Kakazu Ridge and running its entire length was a deep gorge cut into the coral by the immemorial passage of a narrow stream. The gorge was a natural antitank obstacle, impassable to tracked vehicles. For tanks to attempt to turn either flank of the ridge would bring down on them a storm of artillery.

Finally, Colonel Hara had emplaced outposts in tombs and concrete pillboxes on the ridge's northern face. Most effective of all, he had cleverly emplaced most of his infantry and all of his mortars on the southern or reverse slope of the ridge. They were thus in untouchable defilade, shielded from enemy troops, artillery, and even American battleships. Not even enemy mortars, with that weapon's high, looping trajectory, could reach them. Moreover, the Americans were absolutely unaware of this reverse-slope concentration; while Hara, of course, had his entire front registered by his own guns.

Thus, Kakazu Ridge.

Colonel May was sometimes called "a soldier of the old school"—meaning that he believed that the brave charge could usually carry the day. This does not suggest that he would not maneuver, only that faced by such a forbidding unflankable position, he would instinctively fall back on the frontal assault. So he ordered two of his three battalions to storm Kakazu Ridge and Kakazu West on April 9, actually expecting both to fall by the following morning. This meant that—in accordance with American infantry doctrine—a battalion of three companies would use two of them in attack with the third in reserve, and thus, two companies would strike the main ridge and two more Kakazu West, with the remaining two on call in their rear. To achieve surprise, there would be no artillery preparation beforehand, and all units would attack before daylight.

Right at the start one of the companies assaulting Kakazu West was late moving out and did not march until daylight, when it was sighted and promptly pinned down. The other company was commanded by a born fighter and leader, First Lieutenant Willard Mitchell, a powerfully built southerner who had played both football and basketball for Mississippi State. Idolized by his

men and called "Captain Hoss," he was also beloved for his un-
bashful battle cry: "Watch out! Here comes 'the Hoss'—and God
is on the Hoss's side!" Mitchell returned their affection by calling
them his "Lardasses," a fondly derisive and droll nickname that
they loved.

Mitchell's Lardasses were quick to ascend Kakazu West under
cover of darkness, and not particularly dismayed to learn that they
were alone on its crest and that their supporting comrades were
pinned down below. They also found that the position was composed of two knolls—one on the north, and the other to the
south, forming Colonel Hara's reverse slope. Between them was
a shallow saddle of land. The moment that the Japanese emerged
from their steel-and-coral fortress, Mitchell quickly formed his
company into a perimeter on the saddle, just deep enough to
conceal a prone man. He hoped to riddle them if they charged
forward to clear both saddle and northward knoll. But the enemy
refused to oblige, opening fire from their own position and showering the saddle with hand grenades and satchel charges, bags
stuffed with explosive. Mitchell's men fought back with the same
weapons, and a furious battle raged back and forth all morning
long—with men killed and wounded on both sides.

Throughout the action, Mitchell roved the besieged saddle,
hurling grenades and firing his carbine, his battle cry booming
from his lips. His men were his gallant equal, and one of them
—Pfc. Joseph Solch—spotted an enemy spigot mortar mounted
in a cave on the reverse slope. Just one of its 320 mm shells could
destroy the Americans on the saddle. With Captain Hoss, Solch
and his buddies attacked the huge mortar, destroying it with hand
grenades and killing its nine-man crew.

At about noon, sensing that the Americans had but a small
force in front of him, Colonel Hara ordered his men to make a
series of four furious counter-attacks on the enemy. So that they
might surprise the Americans, and with brutal indifference to
their destruction or survival, he sent them charging through his

own mortar fire. Lieutenant Bill Curran killed both the leaders of the first charge, while his men repulsed the Japanese with heavy loss. When a second assault came, Solch, squatting on his haunches, fired his Browning Automatic Rifle (BAR) from the hip to repel an entire company. In the final charge, the Japanese—throwing "satchel charges as big as boxes of apples"—came within a few feet of overrunning the "American devils" but finally fell a few feet short.

Even so, Mitchell's company was being badly whittled. Because his soldiers were lying on hard coral, they could not get below ground by scooping out foxholes, and thus were inviting targets for enemy riflemen and exposed to the flame and fragments of exploding mortar shells.

Fierce fighting also raged atop Kakazu Ridge to the east, or left of Mitchell's position. Here the Japanese popped in and out of their barricaded caves to strike the men of companies led by Captain Jack Royster and First Lieutenant Dave Belman. They also charged up the reverse slope, again braving their own mortars. An entire American platoon was pinned down by a pair of enemy machine guns. Pfc. Edward Moskala crawled toward them, clutching his BAR. When close enough but still unobserved, he hurled grenades at the unsuspecting Japanese, rising to rush them spraying bullets. Both guns were knocked out.

Now Lieutenant Belman was hit, refusing evacuation despite great loss of blood. Captain Royster took a mortar fragment in the face. In exquisite pain and nearly blind, he also refused to leave. But it was becoming plain to both officers that the enemy was gaining the upper hand. GIs had already begun to withdraw off the ridge crest, hunting protection in the numerous caves and holes on the ridge's northern face. After Royster radioed battalion for help, Lieutenant Colonel King ordered another company to the rescue. But this unit got no farther than the gorge, crouching with the men who had been pinned down there since sunup. King now believed that his battalion was in trouble and asked May for permission to withdraw. May refused, telling King that he'd lose as many men withdrawing as he would holding the hill. He also told him that if he was "jumpy, have the executive officer take over." Understandably, there was no reply.

Captain Royster on the ridge had a far better appreciation of his danger than either hard-boiled Eddy May or the cautious Colonel King. His and Belman's company could not possibly retreat in full view of the enemy. So Royster called for smoke shells from the Eighty-eighth Chemical Mortar Battalion. They went humming up and looping down, but the wind blew them back into Royster's face. Eventually there was enough smoke to conceal a withdrawal, and the GIs began crawling down toward the gorge, many of them carrying wounded buddies with them. Ed Moskala was the last man down, but when he learned that a wounded man unable to move was still atop the ridge, he went back up to bring him safely down.

Now the remnants of King's entire battalion were pinned down in the gorge, immobilized by enemy fire. To leap erect was to die. Second Lieutenant Leo Ford, the officer now in charge, decided that the best way out was to creep down the defile to the jump-off point of Hoss Mitchell's company earlier in the day. Snaking along inch by inch on their bellies, dragging their wounded, Ford and his men moved westward at a snail's pace. Ed Moskala, who had volunteered again to act as rear guard, covered their withdrawal. Twice he rescued wounded buddies, but on his second trip he paid for his gallantry with his life. For these acts of infinite compassion, and his bravery in destroying the enemy guns, Moskala received the posthumous award of the Medal of Honor.

By four in the afternoon, the men led by Ford reached a point opposite the north slope of Kakazu West, and were soon joined by Mitchell's GIs moving rapidly under billowing smoke skillfully called down by Captain Hoss himself.

The Kakazu attack had failed, but it had not been a disaster.

In all, Colonel May's 383rd Regiment had suffered 326 casualties, with 23 dead, 47 missing and presumed dead, plus 256 wounded. Colonel Hara's command may have lost half of its strength of 1,200; and for the defenders to lose nearly twice as many as the attackers, while fighting from a most formidable fixed position, testifies to the valor and skill of the American infantry.

Even before the failure at Kakazu became known at Ninety-sixth Division headquarters, Brigadier Claudius Easley, assistant commander of the Ninety-sixth, had prepared a second much more massive assault under his personal command. This "powerhouse attack" with no attempt at surprise was to be spearheaded by four battalions of infantry—about three thousand soldiers—supported by eight battalions of 105 and 155 mm artillery, together with air strikes and bombardment from the sea led by the battleship *New York*. There would be no tanks once again, for that gorge below the ridge was still impassable.

At 7:15 A.M. on April 10 the assault began. Furious as the preliminary bombardment had been, it in no way depleted Ushijima's troop strength. When the bombardment lifted, his men—safe and invisible within his steel-and-coral fortress—would reply with small arms, machine guns, mortars, and occasionally one of those huge 624-pound mortar shells. Once again the Ninety-sixth fought gallantly, but flesh-and-blood advancing in the open, no matter how valiantly, simply cannot overcome an unseen enemy firing from within underground fortifications of steel and coral. It was almost as though the Japanese and the Americans had exchanged battle doctrines: the defenders relying upon firepower and the invaders on spiritual power, with the inevitable consequence: The Americans were stopped. Fortunately for them, a heavy rain—the forerunner of drenching downpours soon to come—squelched the battle, or their casualties might have been greater.

It required two more days of hideous combat to convince General Easley that Kakazu was simply too formidable for the Ninety-sixth to conquer alone. On April 11 Colonel John Cassidy's battalion of the 381st Regiment made its second attempt to seize the top of the ridge and was again driven back. That night the Japanese began bombarding the Americans pinned down in the gorge with their 320 mm spigot mortars. One of these huge projectiles, woefully inaccurate and fired so haphazardly, seemingly did strike harmlessly on the ground—but with enough force to start a landslide that buried a cave being used as an aid station, killing thirteen Americans and wounding nine.

On the morning of the twelfth, Easley ordered another attack by Cassidy's battalion, supported by heavy air strikes. When the Ninety-sixth moved out, there fell upon them a shower of mortar shells so thick that they came down at the rate of better than sixty a minute. Forty-five men were lost, and that was the end of the Kakazu debacle of April 9–12.

During the failed April 9–12 assaults the only appreciable gains made by the Twenty-fourth Corps was by the veteran Seventh Infantry Division on the left or eastern flank of the Ninety-sixth. From Triangulation Hill to Ouki on Nakagusuku Bay, the Seventh drove forward one thousand yards. Ouki fell to the Thirty-second Infantry on April 11, but the Americans were promptly evicted. By the night of April 12 all of the Seventh's formations were halted in front of Hill 178, a towering crag in roughly the center-east of Ushijima's line, which was also a Japanese artillery observation point. Farther east the Ninety-sixth's 382nd Regiment had been stopped cold at Tombstone Ridge, where on April 11 it went into defensive positions. Tombstone may have been every bit as tough as Kakazu, but no assault was planned until General Hodge and his division commanders could assess the situation.

Casualties in the Seventh and Ninety-sixth divisions had been

451 dead, with 241 missing and presumed dead and 2,198 wounded, for a total of 2,890. Enemy losses were estimated at 5,750—all killed—although this was almost certainly exaggerated. A truer figure more likely would be about 4,000. Most of these men were killed by bombardment, for during April 9–12 the American invaders had hurled a massive weight of metal from land, sea, and air upon the defending Japanese. The fact that Kakazu, Tombstone, and Ouki remained in enemy hands demonstrated to the American commanders that the key to success on Okinawa lay in possession of the reverse slopes of all those ridges from Kakazu to Shuri Castle. Seizing the forward slopes, though difficult, could be done—but any attempt to drive past them would bring upon the attackers that dreadful rain of enemy fire.

What was needed, it seemed to General Hodge, was even heavier bombardments—and there was not yet enough ammunition ashore. The loss of those two ammunition ships to the *kamikaze*, deemed not critical at first, was now one of the chief causes of delay. Kakazu would have to wait until enough 105 and 155 mm shells had come across the beaches to make sustained daily shelling a reality. Already, after only about nine days of battle, it had become apparent that the Okinawa campaign would depend upon supply as much as battle.

Back to *Banzai!*

CHAPTER TWELVE

Reports of the Battle of Kakazu Ridge were received by Lieutenant General Isamu Cho (he had received another star) and Colonel Hiromichi Yahara with predictable reactions. Although neither knew the exact number of enemy fallen or even their own losses, Yahara was eminently pleased with the result. The Americans had been dealt a bloody repulse exactly as he had planned in his defense-in-depth tactics, and soon the rate of attrition among them would so whittle the Tenth Army that the Americans would cancel their offensive so that not only the homeland would be saved, but Okinawa as well.

To General Cho it appeared that the enemy had suffered grievously and was so rocked back on their heels that the time had come for a full-scale offensive of the Thirty-second Army. Since his humiliation in the earlier showdown between him and Yahara, when General Ushijima had sided with his planning chief, the fiery Cho had not ceased to press for a counter-attack. But even his friend and mentor Ushijima remained unmoved, until an order from Imperial Headquarters was received urging the Thirty-second Army to overrun Yontan and Kadena Airfields.

This was probably the result of a Japanese intelligence warning that Marine Corsairs would soon arrive at these airfields in strength and would make the mission of the various *kikusui* more difficult than ever. Cho seized on this directive to persuade Ushijima on April 6 to order an attack prepared for April 8. But the ever-alert Yahara pounced upon the appearance of a 110-ship convoy offshore of the Urasoe-Mura Escarpment on April 7 as proof that the Americans were going to strike the Sixty-second Division on its flank. Alarmed, Ushijima for the second time canceled a Cho-sponsored assault.

But then both the American failure at Kakazu Ridge and the "remarkable" destruction wrought upon the enemy fleet by the first of the *kikusui* convinced Ushijima and Cho that the time to strike had indeed come. This misconception was strengthened by "a stirring telegraph order" from Naval Headquarters claiming that *Ten-Go* had been "very successful." "There are signs of uneasiness among enemy forces and odds are seven to three in our favor." Everyone involved in the Okinawa defense should unite in "a general pursuit operation."

Isamu Cho, though not as rational as his rival Yahara, was at least as clever. Everywhere he seemed to see signs of enemy weakness, among them slackening aerial activity on April 10, as well as a Navy report of a reduction in the number of American ships in the Hagushi Anchorage. The calculating Yahara could have explained the first as a result of the same cloudy, rainy weather that discomfited everyone on the island—Cho included —and the second as caused by the visible stream of unloaded enemy ships sailing back to base for reloading and return. But Cho was then at his argumentative best, and over the precise but uninspiring protests of the unhappy Yahara, General Ushijima ordered a "powerful" counter-attack for the night of April 12–13.

Cho's plan was for massive infiltration of almost the entire east-west front of the U.S. Seventh and Ninety-sixth Divisions. Three battalions of the Japanese Twenty-fourth Division would strike the Seventh on the east (or right of the American line), while three more from the Sixty-second Division would assault the battered Ninety-sixth. They would, of course, attack at night, a Japanese preference born of a desire to negate that dreaded American artillery. Breaking through the advance American units, the troops would then spread out in the rear area to a point four miles below Kadena Airfield. There they would take refuge in known caves and tombs. On the morning of April 13 they would emerge to slaughter Tenth Army's rear-echelon troops, usually technical, headquarters, supply, and soldiers armed with nothing more lethal than a pencil. In the mêlée that would ensue, troops of both sides would be so hopelessly intermixed that the enemy would not dare to bring his artillery, air, and naval gunfire to bear. Meanwhile, other battalions remaining in place opposite the Seventh and Ninety-sixth would launch a furious attack intended to compel the Yankees to retreat, perhaps in such panic that they would be included in the general slaughter of the enemy's rear echelon. Cho did not specify what would happen next, whether he intended actually to overrun the airfields as Imperial Headquarters had suggested, destroying installations and aircraft at will, or would be content merely with unnerving Buckner and disorganizing his two forward divisions.

With troops marching in drenching rain to their jump-off positions on April 12, Hiromichi Yahara became so apprehensive that he committed an act of insubordination so incredible that in any Western army it could not have ended otherwise than in a court-martial and dismissal—or perhaps worse. He went to Lieutenant General Takeo Fujioka, commander of the Sixty-second Division, and Lieutenant General Tatsumi Amamiya, commander of the Twenty-fourth, and actually persuaded them not to use three battalions each in the forthcoming operation, but only two.

Not six, but four battalions would march to the plan of Isamu Cho.

Three flares burst over Kakazu Ridge during the early darkness of April 12. Two were red, the first signaling, "Commence artillery fire," and the other, "We are attacking with full strength tonight"; and the third, shaped like a dragon, was for "Make all-out attack." Almost instantly, at about 7 P.M., there fell on the Americans the heaviest Japanese artillery concentration of the war. On the sector of the battered Ninety-sixth alone about twenty-two hundred rounds exploded, while within five minutes another two hundred rocked the Seventh's zone. Fortunately these Yankees with their painfully acquired battle savvy had dug their holes so "dry and deep" that few casualties resulted.

First to strike the Americans was the Twenty-second Infantry Regiment, which had marched for two days in pouring rain from its base on Oroku Peninsula just south of Naha. Loaded down with 110-pound packs and bags of food—an immense burden for these normally small soldiers—they had been told by their commander, Lieutenant Colonel Masaru Yoshida, to move in "a sinuous eel line," and they did indeed feel more like fish than flesh as they lay huddled and shivering in cane fields to escape detection by enemy air. By nightfall they were already dispirited and bewildered, moving over unfamiliar terrain and with no precise plan. Instead of attacking en masse, they sought to infiltrate the Seventh Division's sector in twos or threes or a squad or two, but got nowhere. One massed attack of about a hundred Japanese was riddled by GIs firing rifles and machine guns, killing about a third of them, wounding another third, and compelling all survivors to take refuge in a cave.

The assault on the Ninety-sixth Division's front, however, was much heavier, better organized, and of longer duration—personally directed as it was by General Fujioka. Guileful and stealthy as always, a long column of Japanese sought to penetrate the Ninety-sixth's position by pretending to be GIs marching openly down Highway 5 in a column of twos. Twenty of them slipped past scrutiny until the Americans, realizing that they were not friendly troops on their flank, opened fire with all weapons. Those who survived scurried for cover in caves and tombs, but fifty-eight of their comrades were left dead on the field. Two more attacks were mounted against the Ninety-sixth, but both failed with heavy loss.

General Fujioka next tried to roll up his enemy with two companies following an artillery barrage against Kakazu Ridge. A small force staged a diversion around the western flank of Kakazu West while the main body tried to overrun the draw between that point and Kakazu Ridge. First to meet them was Pfc. William Daily at the trigger of a heavy machine gun in the draw. Unable to depress his gun enough to strike the approaching enemy below him, Daily began tossing grenades. Their explosions alerted Staff Sergeant Beauford "Snuffy" Anderson, holed up in a tomb with his light mortar section. Anderson left the tomb to hurl all of his grenades at the Japanese, and then emptied his carbine. Glancing about him, his eye fell on a dud enemy mortar. Seizing it he spiraled it football-style into the draw and was rewarded by an explosion and screams. Rushing back into the tomb he collected his own mortars, wrenched them from their casings, yanked out the safety pins, slamming the shell against a rock to release the setback pin, and spiraled this heavier and more lethal "football" into the draw. Again an explosion and screams . . . With this impromptu "passing attack," Anderson sent all of his fifteen lethal footballs spinning into the darkness below, and by this effective exercise in Yankee battle ingenuity he stopped an entire enemy platoon. In the morning he counted twenty-five enemy bodies, plus seven abandoned knee mortars and four machine guns. For his bravery and quickness of thought, Anderson received the Medal of Honor.

Other Japanese who had infiltrated Kakazu West met the
same end. When an enemy officer approached a BAR man and
asked him if he were Japanese, the GI snorted, "No!"—and shot
him dead, along with ten of his men following in single file. Soldiers of a company command post under attack in a tomb sallied
forth to kill twenty Japanese. On the western slope of Kakazu
West a single American machine gunner mowed down twenty-
three more sons of Nippon.

Another enemy force nearly broke through the draw, until
they were illuminated by star shells fired over the battlefield by
American warships offshore, a technique developed at Peleliu and
so successful that night actually could be turned into day. Silhou-
etted against the dark, the enemy was easily riddled and their
attack broken in blood. Dawn revealed a draw covered with
sprawling corpses.

General Cho's desperation attack was also hurled back on
Kakazu Ridge proper. When the Ninety-sixth's heavy mortar
crews were informed that about forty Japanese were threatening
to overrun their battalion observation post, they decided to risk
close support of their riflemen buddies up front. Hoping that
their comrades would be safely below ground in pits and foxholes,
they sent about eight hundred high-explosive shells humming
skyward, to come plunging straight down with a horrible whistling noise that was the last sound many Japanese ever heard.
Marine artillery also joined the bombardment, firing shells that
drew a curtain of explosives around the endangered position. In
the morning enemy dead were "stacked like cordwood" below.

In their headquarters below Shuri Castle a sorrowing General
Ushijima and a despairing General Cho heard nothing but de-
pressing reports from the front. Nevertheless, it was still hoped
that a battalion of the Twenty-second Regiment that had slipped
through American lines undetected to enter the Ginowan area
might hide out in caves until daybreak, when they could emerge
to shoot up the American rear echelons—and even perhaps reach

Yontan and Kadena to destroy enemy aircraft. But in scattering for sanctuary during the night, they had become so fragmented that daybreak showed them incapable of concerted action. So they remained hidden until nightfall of the thirteenth, when half of them successfully slipped back into their own lines. Two final Japanese counter-attacks were repulsed during the early-morning darkness of the fourteenth, one of them with losses of 116 men, closing out Isamu Cho's abortive counter-offensive.

It had not, of course, been a proper *Banzai!*: howling, *sake*-crazed troops, screaming and screeching as they ran through the darkness banging canteens on bayonets and yelling in singsong English what they presumed to be blood-curdling oaths—"Japanese boy drink American boy's blood!"—only to be herded into enemy barbed wire by American mortars falling behind them, there to be riddled or sometimes even exterminated by accurate machine-gun and rifle fire. But it was still a reversion to bamboo-spear tactics, and worse, a decision to come outside of the caves and tombs and pillboxes from which they had successfully halted the two-division advance of General Hodge's Twenty-fourth Corps, and expose themselves to the devastation of overwhelmingly superior American artillery, mortar, and naval gunfire, as well as accurate small arms. Ushijima, in authorizing this romantic regression into the failed tactics of the past, had blessed an operation ill conceived, understrength, misdirected, haphazard, and uncoordinated. As a result, more than half the force involved—1,594 men—were killed. To approve a plan calling for splendid defensive fighters to take the offensive at night while moving over unfamiliar terrain and woefully inferior in numbers and firepower was simply to grasp the muzzle of military success rather than the pistol grip; and also to surrender his own enormous advantage in terrain and tenacious troops: natural obstacles made unassailable by improved fortifications, thus canceling out his enemy's superior firepower, and manned by invisible troops movable only in death.

He did this because, like Isamu Cho, his heart had conquered his head; and because most Japanese commanders from Midway-Guadalcanal to Okinawa itself could never shed that *Bushido*-born, carefully cultivated conviction that the soft, spoiled, luxury-loving Americans would quail at the first flash of a *Samurai* saber.

Kikusui 2:
Kamikaze Crucible

CHAPTER THIRTEEN

Admiral Matome Ugaki was still convinced that his April 6–7 strikes at the Americans had seriously damaged TF 58, an estimate not shared by his colleague, Lieutenant General Michio Sugahara of the Sixth Air Army. A report made by Sugahara's staff somewhat sourly concluded: "Despite many attacks, the Navy cannot block the enemy's carrier force, which still is operating east of Okinawa."

Nevertheless Sugahara was eminently cooperative in preparing for *Kikusui 2*, which Ugaki hoped would so shatter Spruance's fleet that it might seek sanctuary in the open sea. But both he and the army general realized that the second Floating Chrysanthemum would never equal the strength of the first, if only because of the serious losses it had suffered. They were also concerned to learn that Marine Corsairs had indeed arrived at Yontan and Kadena, thus menacing their own aircraft with ground-based fighters that, because of their proximity to their base, were more to be feared than carrier-based interceptors.

Their apprehension was somewhat eased, however, with the arrival on Kyushu of a new weapon: the *Oka*, or "Cherry Blossom" glide bomb, a rocket-boosted, piloted suicider capable of speeds of 500 knots and carrying a huge wallop of 2,645 pounds of trinitroanisol. The *Oka* was slung beneath a mother plane, usually a heavy Betty or Peggy bomber, and flown to within about a dozen miles of its target, when it was released with the pilot firing its rockets and directing it toward its target. Moving at pistol-bullet speed, the *Oka* was believed to be almost immune to enemy gunfire, but its very velocity made it extremely difficult for its pilot to keep his 16½-foot missile on target. American intelligence was aware of the appearance of this new weapon, but considered it so ineffective that it was christened *baka*, or "foolish."

Although *Kikusui 2* was scheduled for April 12, Admiral Ugaki tried to destroy "the remnant" of TF 58 on the day before, hurling a daylight suicide attack of about fifty-two planes against Admiral Mitscher's carrier force. Typically glowing reports claimed three carriers sunk, a cruiser set ablaze, another cruiser holed, and two destroyers hit with torpedoes. The next day Ugaki's pilots, still mightier with pen than bomb, reported sinking two battleships and a light cruiser. Actually very little damage was done to Mitscher's ships on either day. Some damage was inflicted on the veteran flattop *Enterprise*, and a *kamikaze* crashed the majestic new battleship *Missouri*, but succeeded only in scratching her deck and blistering some paint. Destroyer *Kidd* was hit on picket duty and badly hurt, with thirty-eight sailors killed and fifty-five wounded, the worst casualty of the day. Waggish bluejackets aboard another picket destroyer, exasperated by repeated strikes at their station, erected a huge sign on deck with an arrow pointing aft and reading: CARRIERS THIS WAY.

Both Ugaki and Sugahara hoped to neutralize the enemy Corsairs by planning a series of bombing raids on their airfields the night before the scheduled attacks of April 12, while Sugahara also organized a decoy flight of fighters to lure TF 58's Hellcats and Corsairs away from the impact area. In the bombing operation, 22 Japanese aircraft struck Yontan and Kadena shortly before dawn of the twelfth, damaging 5 enemy planes but losing 5 of their own to American gunners of all services. Next, Sugahara's decoys attracted nothing but birds rising for dawn breakfasts, so that it was not until eleven o'clock in the morning that the Kyushu main body of about 120 late-model fighters arrived over both Kikai Jima and the Hagushi Anchorage to try to clear the strike area for following flights of 76 *kamikaze*, plus 20 suiciders roaring up from Formosa.

Although the Nipponese fighters were more successful than usual against the more skillful Americans flying better planes—claiming a probably exaggerated 20 kills—the Navy and Marine pilots from the carriers of TF 58 reported a much higher 126 enemy planes downed during fighter sweeps. This also was probably exaggerated—not by intent like the starry-eyed enemy—but from the inevitable duplication occurring when more than one fighter was firing on the same enemy, or even when a "flamer" plunging toward a watery grave might have the winds caused by his velocity blow the fires out, enabling him to return successfully to base. "Kill" estimates like body counts were much like American taxpayers' income-tax returns: so full of deductions for charity that the churches of America would all be rich "beyond the dreams of avarice."

But the American interceptors did effectively prevent the enemy fighters from protecting the *kamikaze*. Although the suiciders succeeded in damaging eight American ships—mostly destroyers and destroyer-escorts of the radar picket line, as well as some smaller craft—and causing high casualities, only one warship was sunk: the new picket destroyer *Manert L. Abele*, the first kill on record by a *baka* bomb.

Abele was on Picket Station 14 about thirty miles west of Okinawa when it was jumped by a pair of suicide Vals. *Abele*'s AA opened up, each burst seemingly scoring a hit but with the

planes reappearing through the smoke. One of the attackers was
sent into the sea, but the second struck the destroyer's after engine room, spreading death and destruction and causing *Abele* to
buckle visibly. Just then one of two Betty bombers circling like
scavengers overhead released its *baka* bomb, which came shrieking
at the stricken destroyer at five hundred knots. The pilot kept his
missile perfectly on course, striking *Abele* exactly amidships. A
tremendous blast lifted the American out of the water to be
slammed back again. Many men were blown overboard, among
them Lieutenant s.g. George Wray, who swam back to his ship,
clambering aboard to tear open a jammed escape hatch allowing
the entire watch of the forward engine room to scramble to safety.
In less than another minute, Wray might have been too late, for
Abele sank five minutes after the *baka* struck. Most of her officers
and crew were rescued by a nearby LSM, but six men were killed
and seventy-three missing.

Simultaneous with the agony of *Abele*, a flight of conventional
kamikaze found Rear Admiral Deyo's gunfire support force patrolling waters off the Motobu Peninsula. When they struck,
Deyo fortunately had his ships concentrated and they were ready
for the Divine Winds, which could do little more than stagger a
destroyer and crash a 40 mm mount aboard battleship *Tennessee*.
One sailor who was blown into the air landed atop a five-inch
gun turret, where he crouched while calmly stripping off his
burning clothing to await a cold bath from the nearest fire hose.
Marine Corporal W. H. Putnam either fell or was blown overboard, surfacing near a big life raft. He clambered aboard, finding
unusual company in the presence of the headless torso of the
kamikaze who had crashed his ship.

Thus the scourging of the American fleet off Okinawa continued unabated, but once again the *kamikaze* had failed to strike
the paralyzing blow so eagerly sought by Admiral Ugaki. Losses
among the suiciders are not exactly known, although 185 of them

had participated in the assault—an enormous decline from the 355 making the first attacks. The decrease would continue until on June 21–22 Ugaki could scrape together only 45 decrepit Divine Winds—the shriveled petals remaining on the deadly Floating Chrysanthemums.

Uncle Sam:
Logistics Magician

CHAPTER FOURTEEN

Triumphs of logistics, though impressive, usually do not make "rattling good reading," as one British historian wrote of the Napoleonic Wars. Yet the industrial and logistics feat of the United States of America fighting the first great two-ocean war on record is unrivaled in the history of humankind; and at Okinawa during the culminating battle of the Island War, as well as the greatest amphibious operation in military annals, the Americans had to overcome two unprecedented challenges.

First, it had to supply this unrivaled sea invasion at a distance of seventy-five hundred miles from its western shores. Second, it had to keep a fleet unsurpassed in numbers of ships and firepower constantly at sea for weeks at a time while feeding it with ammunition, food, fuel, airplanes, and those myriad lesser demands of an invader engaged on land and sea and in the air.

Even more than Admiral Spruance's Fifth Fleet and Mitscher's Task Force Fifty-eight, General Buckner's Tenth Army was a monster of consumption. Between April 1 and 16 alone, no less than 577,000 tons of supplies were landed on the Hagushi Beaches, a record achieved in the face of two destructive storms and the attacks of the *kamikaze*. A difficulty unsuspected by the *Iceberg* planners—though actually a happy one—was the incredible speed of the advance of Buckner's attacking divisions, so rapid that Ducks and amphibious tractors expecting to haul their supplies no farther than the beaches were obliged to roll far inland to unload.

Another problem caused by unforeseen success was that because planners had placed the unloading priority of spare vehicles lower than such vital supplies as ammunition, barbed wire, fuel, and food, these first-priority supplies had to be heaped on the beaches to get at the now-sorely-needed jeeps and trucks. This caused the breakdown of an elaborate plan for supply dumps to be established at carefully selected points. Night unloading under floodlights, suspended only during air-raid alerts, helped to unload waiting ships speedily, but also added to beach congestion.

On April 13 General Buckner was dismayed to learn that during the past twenty-four hours only 640 tons of artillery ammunition had crossed the beaches, not nearly enough to supply guns expending more shells than planners had anticipated. Buckner immediately gave priority to artillery shells, and in the next few days 3,000 tons daily were deposited ashore—enough not only for those tireless guns but also to begin building a reserve.

Okinawa's "excellent network of bad roads"—all narrow and lightly surfaced—could not be traversed by American armored tractors and six-by-six trucks. Those early April rainstorms that had delayed unloading of ships also made the roads softer, compelling American engineers to try to harden them with sand mixed with coral. But the coral was not easy to dig and had to be blasted frequently. Without a rock crusher, the engineers sometimes dumped coral fragments as big as boulders on the roads, turning some of them into obstacle courses.

Erection of numerous pontoon causeways from the reefs to solid ground helped ease the continuing problem of moving supplies from ship to shore. LCTs—Landing Craft, Tank—and

LSMs could tie up to the small ones, transferring their cargo directly into trucks. The bigger ships at the bigger causeways used cranes. Red Beach 1 opposite Yontan Airfield had the largest causeway: 1,428 feet long with a pierhead 45 by 175 feet. During the first few days sixty thousand men and 110,000 tons of cargo crossed the piers.

The most serious shortage was in shells for the 81 mm mortars—those unlovely "stovepipes" that probably have killed more soldiers than any other weapon devised—caused by the loss to *kamikaze* April 6 of those two ammunition ships. But the ever-resourceful Admiral Turner quickly put in an emergency request to Guam, and 117 tons of mortar shells were airlifted to Okinawa, enough to keep the stovepipes firing until many more tons could arrive by ship. Yontan and Kadena Airfields were kept so well supplied that not a single plane was grounded for lack of fuel during the entire campaign.

Fifth Fleet and TF 58 were supplied by a force of cargo ships and oilers commanded by Rear Admiral D. G. Beary from his flagship in the old light cruiser *Detroit*. When Beary received requests from carrier groups for oil and/or ammunition, he would send formations of the necessary ships hurrying to the flattop fleets to begin replenishment at dawn and complete it by dusk. Long before Okinawa, the Navy had perfected the system of refueling at sea, and eventually replacement ships were trained to fill the carriers' every need—even such bulky items as crated airplane engines or jeeps for use on flight decks. Weapons, bombs, and bullets were soon added, and thus at Okinawa TF 58 could remain almost indefinitely at sea—a fact that might be a boon to Admiral Mitscher, but a bore to his "swab-jockeys" weary of sea duty and eager for a little fun ashore. In the immemorial rhythm of "for want of a nail a shoe was lost," the most serious problem was inadequate supplies of 3½- and 4-inch Manila line, and this would not be solved until the Philippines were completely reconquered.

Supply of the bombardment warships off Okinawa was made easy by Admiral Turner's foresight in seizing the Keramas not only for a ship's hospital but also to keep the big naval guns bellowing. A new class of LST ammunition ships equipped with mobile cranes shuttling between the Keramas and Ulithi and the Marianas was able to deposit cargos directly onto the decks of bombardment warships. They also were "type loaded," that is, carrying ammunition for just one class of ship—say, five-inchers and 40 mm for destroyers.

Fuel for all these ships together with about a thousand carrier aircraft was supplied both by Admiral Beary and fleet tankers sailing from Guam to Okinawa or meeting thirsty ships at sea. Two huge fleet tankers left Guam every three days. Every day during the peak period of April 4–24 an average of 167,000 42-gallon barrels of fuel oil was consumed by the ships at and around Okinawa, plus 385,000 gallons of aviation gasoline. By May 27 nearly 9,000,000 barrels of oil had been consumed and 21,000,000 gallons of aviation gasoline, to say nothing of the delivery of less-vital but still-important items as 2,700,000 packages of cigarettes, 1,200,000 candy bars, and over 24,000,000 pieces of mail—to "gladden the heart" of American servicemen there. Suggestive of the extent of the logistical triumph occurring at the Great Loo Choo was the fact that four escort carriers were employed to protect replacement planes and pilots being ferried to the battle area, with seventeen more on the same mission between the West Coast and the Marianas.

Aside from the loss of those two ammunition ships, Japan's naval and air forces did next to nothing to interfere with this enormous supply pipeline. Because Admiral Beary's fleet operated about two hundred miles south of Okinawa with air cover from two escort carriers, it was rarely attacked. One lone *kamikaze* did score a hit on the fleet oiler *Taluga*, but this minor damage was quickly repaired.

Hodge's Hurricane Attack Hurled Back

CHAPTER FIFTEEN

The failure of the Japanese counter-attack on April 12–13 had convinced Major General John Hodge that the time had come for a major breakthrough in Ushijima's Naha-Shuri-Yonabaru line. It was scheduled for April 19.

In the interval, the Seventy-seventh Infantry Division landed on Ie Shima just off the western tip of Motobu Peninsula, about to fall to the Sixth Marine Division. Ie was a fair-sized island with a completed airfield. Landing on April 16, the Seventy-seventh fought a savage four-day battle, killing 4,706 Japanese—many or perhaps even most of them uniformed civilians—while losing 258 soldiers killed or missing and 879 wounded. Marching with the Seventy-seventh was Ernie Pyle.

Before Pyle left Ulithi to join the First Marine Division, another correspondent yelled at him jokingly, "Keep your head down, Ernie." Snorting in disdain, the GI's Friend replied: "Listen, you bastards—I'll take a drink over every one of your graves." But it was Ernie's last resting place that was dug on Ie Shima. As it always was with Pyle, he was at the front—driving there with a battalion commander. Suddenly a Japanese machine gun opened up, and the driver with his two passengers dived into a ditch. After the machine gun fell silent, the commander and Pyle raised their heads—and the gun chattered again. Pyle slumped back into the ditch. Bullets had entered his forehead just below his helmet. Over his grave his new comrades in the Pacific placed a monument with the inscription: "On this spot, the 77th Infantry Division lost a buddy, Ernie Pyle, 18 April, 1945."

Two days later the defending Japanese mounted a desperate counter-attack in an effort to recover ground lost during April 20 to the Americans. After dark that night infiltrators in company strength and in small groups—a total of about 500 men—launched a screeching assault on the front of the 307th Infantry's G Company. Many of them penetrated, actually overrunning a battalion command post, and might have broken through but for the efforts of two machine gunners: Staff Sgt. Anthony Cernawsky and Pfc. Martin May. Both men emptied their heavy machine guns repeatedly until they had no more belts left, after which they struck at the enemy with grenades and carbines, until May was wounded by a mortar shell and the enemy driven off. They returned to the attack, and once again May fought them off—but this time he received his mortal wound, and his Medal of Honor was awarded posthumously.

On the following day General Hodge's bellowing, three-division assault began. Its objective was to penetrate defenses around Shuri to seize the low valley and highway linking Yonabaru on the east coast with the capital of Naha on the west. Admirals Spruance and Turner were eager to seize Naha with its excellent port, the very harbor in which Commodore Perry had cast his anchors en route to opening Japan to world trade.

Even though General Hodge was hopeful, he had no illusions about the formidable positions that his troops would be attacking. "It is going to be really tough," he said. "There are sixty-five thousand to seventy thousand fighting Japs holed up in the south end of the island, and I see no way to get them out except blast them out yard by yard." He also said that because he faced a bristling front without flanks stretching from the Pacific Ocean on the east to the East China Sea on the west, there was simply no opportunity for large-scale maneuver. Instead, Naha-Shuri-Yonabaru had to be cracked by weight of metal.

All previous Pacific War bombardments were surpassed by the concentration of explosives—land, sea, and air—that preceded the attack. Twenty-seven battalions of Army and Marine artillery ranging from 105 mm to 8-inch howitzers—354 pieces in all—produced a barrage of 75 pieces per mile, the proportion increasing as the array moved from east to west. Bursting on the enemy with a horrible roar at dawn of the nineteenth, a rain of howling shells struck Japanese emplacements for twenty minutes to the front of the Seventh and Ninety-sixth Divisions. Six battleships, six cruisers, and nine destroyers firing on call thickened the cannonade with projectiles ranging up to one thousand eight hundred pounds, while 650 Navy and Marine aircraft either flew close-up air support for the waiting troops or punished the enemy's outposts and Ushijima's Shuri headquarters with rockets and one-thousand-pound bombs. Meanwhile, troops boated in transports covered by planes and warships made another feint at the Minatoga Beaches in the south, hoping to draw off some of the enemy's strength. But Ushijima was not deceived and gave no such orders. Instead, he reiterated his instructions to all commanders to keep their men safely below ground. Needless to say, they were strictly obeyed even when, after its opening twenty-minute explosions, the American artillery lifted its fire to begin pummeling the rear areas for ten minutes, while American troops feinted at the Japanese front, hoping to deceive the Japanese into believing the bombardment had ceased and thus lure them above ground. But they still remained invisible, so that when their enemy's fire returned to their front again, no one was caught above ground.

Actually, few Japanese were killed and wounded by this massive artillery assault, even though nineteen thousand shells had been fired at them. Brigadier General Joseph Sheetz commanding Twenty-fourth Corps artillery said that he doubted that as many as 190 Japanese—one for every one hundred shells—had been killed in the bombardment.

Nevertheless, the assault went forward—and began to measure its gains in yards.

At the outset all seemed well. Major General George Griner's Twenty-seventh Division, entering Okinawa combat for the first time, had been assigned a pre-dawn assault on the extreme right flank of the Twenty-fourth's front. Griner hoped to outflank the enemy by a night attack, having read a captured 62nd Division intelligence report stating "the enemy generally fires during the night, but very seldom takes offensive action [then]." In his night attack Griner would have to cross Machinato Inlet and to do this would need to construct bridges and improve the road leading to the water. This could not be done by day, for the Japanese had complete observation of the terrain north of the Urasoe-Mura Escarpment. So the bridges were built farther back, and the engineers trained in assembling them and breaking them down. Meanwhile, a bulldozer was assigned to widen and repair the narrow, shell-pocked little jeep road leading to the inlet.

By day, in full view of the enemy, the bulldozer retrieved upended or mired jeeps, by night the driver worked tirelessly to make the road passable for Griner's troops. Thus, before dawn of the Nineteenth the Twenty-seventh's spearheads did indeed cross Machinato Inlet unseen. With dawn, however, they were detected, and a rain of fire struck them to the ground and kept them there. This was the high point of Hodge's massive, three-division assault. All that the night attack had achieved was to allow the Americans to move undetected over the low ground intervening between their jump-off point and their objective.

Elsewhere the assault did not even get that close. It had been hoped that the new flamethrowing tank assigned to the Seventh Division on the left flank would easily destroy Ushijima's outposts. In essence, the new weapon was an old Sherman tank with a flame spout projecting from inside the barrel of its 75 mm cannon. It fired a stream of fiery fluid of mixed napalm and gasoline. The napalm was a soapy, granular flammable substance that would stick like jelly to whatever it hit: tanks, pillboxes—and men. The flamethrower was the only weapon that terrified the Japanese. First widely used on Peleliu, it was usually carried by a big strong man firing a tube connected to a tank on his back. It sometimes backfired, for a bullet could ignite the tank, incinerating everyone in the vicinity, while charring the man who fired it. Adapted to a tank, it was thought to be much harder to stop than a man.

It seemed so when three of these flame-belching monsters and two regular tanks joined the Seventh's attack and clanked toward the coastal flats dotted with fortified tombs and pillboxes beneath Skyline Ridge. Long, hissing jets of orange flame issued from the mouths of the 75s directed into every opening. Soon clouds of greasy black smoke billowed skyward, and the GIs who had been watching in fascination at this incineration of their enemies cheered wildly. Now possessing a foothold below, the Americans began climbing the ridge—straight into an enemy hurricane. First, preregistered mortars fell upon them flashing and crashing, and then, boiling over the crest of the ridge, charging up from the reverse slope, and even rushing into their own mortars to close with the enemy, came a horde of screaming Japanese hurling grenades and satchel charges. Twice they came in counter-attacks, and each time the GIs clung desperately to their weakening hold on the forward slope.

Higher up on Skyline Ridge other soldiers of the Seventh advanced unmolested for five hundred yards—an ominously easy ascent that should have warned them—but when they moved into ground also preregistered, the same rain of enemy fire stopped

them cold. Pinned down throughout the day, all formations of
the Seventh were retreating into their former positions by shortly
after four o'clock.

They had gained not a yard.

In the center of Hodge's assault the Ninety-sixth Division
found its experience even more frustrating than the Seventh's.
The objective was the Tanabaru-Nishibaru ridge line, which
joined Skyline Ridge, Hill 178, and Kakazu Ridge to form the
zone defended by General Fujioka's Sixty-second Division. Repeated local attacks gained no more than outpost ground. Only
one serious attempt to penetrate enemy defenses was made: by a
platoon led by First Lieutenant Lawrence O'Brien of Colonel
Mickey Finn's Thirty-second Regiment. O'Brien tried to move
onto Skyline Ridge and thence westward to the towering mass of
Hill 178. Apart from an exploding shell that killed one man and
wounded three others, O'Brien's men moved rapidly up Skyline's
steep forward slope, then swung right toward 178. A Japanese
machine gun chattered, and the Americans took refuge in an
abandoned pillbox. From a ridge above, the Japanese hurled grenades and fired knee mortars. O'Brien was pinned down. Major
John Connor, the battalion commander, sent a platoon to the
rescue, but this unit also came under enemy fire so scourging that
only six men of the platoon returned to base alive and un-
wounded. With this Connor recalled O'Brien. In another demonstration of how dangerous the forward slopes of the ridges
could be with the rear slopes unconquered, Connor had lost
eighty men and gained not an inch.

After that first quick nighttime surge over unoccupied ground
on the Twenty-fourth's right flank, the Twenty-seventh Division's sector became a burial ground for American armor. Because
the division's foot soldiers failed to penetrate Kakazu's defenses,
the tanks—thirty of them including three armored flamethrowers

and self-propelled 105 mm howitzers—had no supporting infantry. This left them exposed to the plunging fire of enemy 47 mm antitank guns above them, and the infiltration tactics of Nipponese suicide squads hurling satchel charges, usually against the vehicle's bottom plate. Unfortunately for the Yankee tankers, the Japanese at Kakazu were actually waiting for them—praying for them. One 47 mm gunner named Fujio Takeda knocked out five tanks with six shots at four hundred yards. In all, of the thirty American tanks that attacked, only eight survived. Many of the tankers lived, most of them digging holes beneath their disabled steel monsters and remaining in them undetected for as long as three days. Others were killed when the Japanese pried open their turret lids and dropped grenades in.

It was thus that General Hodge's hurricane attack was hurled back. Failing utterly to break through, it did not obtain a single lodgment or foothold in the enemy's defenses, from which further assaults might be mounted. Possibly worse, General Griner in his decision to bypass Kakazu Ridge had left a gap of almost a mile between his Twenty-seventh Division and the Ninety-sixth in the center. No American troops were there to blunt any enemy counter-attack, and so General Hodge worried that a Japanese counter-strike could slip through to trap the entire Twenty-seventh, pressing it against the iron enemy defenses it had failed to pierce and there destroy it. Fortunately, those well-entrenched Japanese were as blind as the moles they resembled, having no idea of their foe's whereabouts, and no enemy counter-attack was launched. Nevertheless, General Griner the next day reiterated his belief that the Japanese strongpoints should be bypassed and mopped up. In reply, Colonel "Screaming Mike" Halloran, commander of the 381st Infantry, gave a more accurate estimate of the enemy's troops: "You cannot bypass a Japanese because a Jap does not know when he is bypassed."

Thus ended the hurricane assault with Twenty-fourth Corps losses totaling 750 killed, missing, and wounded.

Outer Line Cracked/
Ushijima Retreats

CHAPTER SIXTEEN

It was an entirely different American infantryman who wearily and warily greeted the dawn of April 20 on Okinawa. Up until the fiery failure at Kakazu during April 12–13 and the bloody repulse of April 19 at Shuri's outer defenses, the Army infantry in the Pacific—apart from a few isolated instances and during only two major battles, Saipan and Guam—had been fighting a war in which maneuver was possible.

These were on the great land mass of New Guinea, the second largest island in the world, and the Philippine archipelago with its thousands of islands big and small. In these campaigns, maneuver was not only possible but mandatory if casualties were to be kept minimal, and the enemy being attacked was usually fighting from log-and-mud fortifications, half naked and half starved by the effectiveness with which the submarines and warships of the United States Navy had severed their supply lines. The casualties were indeed minimal—as the boastful Douglas MacArthur would trumpet to the world in his tireless pursuit of supreme command in the Pacific—and the Army infantry had few if any days such as the crucibles at Kakazu and before Shuri.

But now—though dimly—the GIs realized that they had come to their own Tarawa, Peleliu, or Iwo Jima with their fortifications of steel, concrete, and coral, interconnected by mazes of tunnels with interlocking fire and all approaches preregistered by every weapon. They now knew—as the Marines in the Central Pacific had learned—that enormous massed bombardment of these truly formidable defenses from sea, air, and land was usually if not always no more effective than a smoke screen. True, they would cause some casualties, but never enough to be decisive; and the accident of a lucky hit could never be repeated *on call*. Only the impetuous foot soldier slashing in with his hand weapons and using tanks, hurling explosives and aiming flame, can succeed in a war against armed and resolute moles. The naval shell's flat trajectory, the bomb's broad parabola, the artillery projectile's arc—even the loop of the mortar—cannot chase such moles down a tunnel. If they can occasionally collapse the whole position with a direct hit, a rare feat, they have knocked out only one spoke in the enemy's wheel. But the wheel still turns, killing and maiming, and again in the absence of that military miracle—direct hits *on call*—the man on foot has to go in. Too often even without his tanks.

Moreover, the losses in armor and the casualties among the American GIs on that near-disastrous April 19 were not only the result of attacks made into Ushijima's clever and sometimes-invisible defenses spouting death and destruction, but also complicated by the terrain of southern Okinawa itself. It was, as the Army's official history states: "ground utterly without pattern; it was a confusion of little, mesa-like hilltops, deep draws, rounded clay hills, gentle green valleys, bare and ragged coral ridges, lumpy mounds of earth, narrow ravines and sloping finger ridges extending downward from the hill masses."

On April 20, General Hodge's three-division assault into Ushijima's meat grinder was renewed: Seventh on left, Ninety-sixth in the center, and Twenty-seventh on the right. In these first two formations the GIs, now thoroughly blooded in this type of warfare, moved forward more warily and skillfully. The Thirty-second Infantry of the Seventh, or "Hour Glass," took Ouki Hill with surprising ease, and then struck at Skyline Ridge, blanketing it with smoke to blind the numerous enemy mortarmen there. The tactic worked, especially after two gallant soldiers—First Lieutenant John Holms and Staff Sergeant James McCarthy—led a final charge to seize the hill, but later perished in a fierce enemy counter-attack that was hurled back. Flamethrowing tanks were of major assistance in this action, burning out a forward mortar position that could have been troublesome.

But the Skyline's dogged defenders did not submit so tamely. One machine gunner in a pillbox was particularly tenacious until Sergeant Theodore MacDonnell, a mortar observer not expected to join a battle, entered the struggle on his own, charging the pillbox throwing grenades. Next he borrowed a BAR, and when that jammed, a carbine—rushing the enemy position with this ordinarily most useless weapon in the American arsenal. At close range, however, it could do damage, and MacDonnell used it to kill all three gunners. Then, his Celtic blood aroused, he picked up the enemy gun and heaved it down the embankment, followed by a knee mortar. Without pausing to thank MacDonnell for this distinguished favor, one of Colonel Finn's companies proceeded to clear Skyline at a cost of two killed and eleven wounded. Hill 178 now came under American fire, and after two days patrols blasting enemy caves found these positions stuffed with corpses: two hundred in one, a hundred in another, fifty in a third, and forty-five in a fourth. Those who had survived had been withdrawn.

The 184th Infantry's objective was the Rocky Crags, two coral pinnacles that had to be taken before towering Hill 178 could be assaulted. But no headway was made the first day. Dismayed, General Arnold came to the front to study these obstacles. Deciding that the crags could be fragmented by direct artillery fire, he ordered a 155 mm howitzer up front. Setting up on a knoll eight hundred yards away and firing over open sights, the crew's first missile—a ninety-five-pound shell with a hardened tip and a concrete-piercing fuse—sent a hefty chunk of coral flying into the air. Seven more destructive shots so upset the Japanese that they sprayed the knoll with machine-gun fire. Two men were wounded, and the survivors quickly dug a hole for their gun. Now unseen, assisted by other guns and flamethrowing tanks, the Americans literally shot both crags into smithereens until both collapsed on themselves.

To the Seventh's right the Ninety-sixth struck at three ridges: Tanabaru-Nishibaru-Tombstone. It took two days of savage fighting to clear Tombstone and to advance to the crest of Nishi-baru. On the night of April 21–22 the Japanese counter-attacked three times against a battalion of the 382nd commanded by Lieutenant Franklin Hartline. In one charge Staff Sergeant David Dovel lifted his machine gun to fire it at the enemy full-trigger, severely burning his hands on the red-hot barrel. Dovel was also wounded in both legs, but survived. Meanwhile soldiers firing light or 60 mm mortars elevated their small stovepipes to a dangerously close eighty-six degrees, dropping shells only thirty yards to their front. Colonel Hartline joined the battle, throwing grenades and firing the weapons of the fallen. At 3:15 A.M. the Japanese retreated, leaving 198 dead comrades behind.

Tanabaru now lay temporarily open, and it was Captain Hoss Mitchell's Lardasses who seized the opportunity. Its earlier losses filled by replacements, the company fought a savage hand-grenade battle that lasted nearly four hours, until Mitchell with three grenades and a carbine rushed the crest to wipe out a machine-gun nest. By nightfall of April 23 the Ninety-sixth held its objectives securely, though it had paid a bloody price of 99 killed and 19 missing with a staggering 660 wounded. Even so, the success of the Seventh and Ninety-sixth clearly indicated to General Hodge that Ushijima's outer line was cracking.

Soldiers of the Twenty-seventh on the twentieth—except for two companies that panicked and fled in disorder when they blundered into an enemy position—were not quite so careful as their comrades in the center and left, probably because they had had a comparatively easy time of it on April 19. Still on the right flank, the New Yorkers moved confidently against a position called Item Pocket, unaware that it was probably Ushijima's toughest and most cleverly designed fortification. Its name derived from its presence in the *I*, or "Item," grid square on the American tactical map. It consisted of coral and limestone ridges running like spokes on a wheel from a swale at its center.

Against it came two battalions of Colonel Gerard Kelly's 165th Infantry, the first commanded by Lieutenant Colonel James Mahoney on the left and the second under Lieutenant Colonel John McDonough on the right. Resisting them was Lieutenant Colonel Kosuke Nishibayashi's Twenty-first Independent Infantry Battalion of about six hundred soldiers together with two or three hundred Okinawan conscripts. All had been working for months on Item's defenses, which they called Gusukuma after a nearby town. There was no safe way to approach the position. Because two bridges on Highway 1 had been knocked out, tanks could not menace it. Every ridge was protected by mortars with machine guns zeroed in from others. Tunnels ran beneath the ridges with openings on either side and on the top. Thus each ridge was a Kakazu in miniature, abundantly stocked with food, ammunition, and water. Until Item fell, there could be no real progress south.

No real attempt to penetrate Item was made on the first day, but on the night of the twenty-first a detail of eight men from McDonough's battalion led by Technical Sergeant Ernest Schoeff tried to seize a ridge in a night attack, and provoked one of the wildest fights of the Okinawa campaign. Forty to fifty Japanese screaming "Banzai!" and hurling grenades charged them from about forty yards away. Scrambling into foxholes that they had dug, Schoeff's men fought back with grenades of their own, rifle shots, rifle butts—even hurling rocks. Pfc. Paul Cook took out ten of the enemy before being killed himself, and when they closed for hand-to-hand fighting, Schoeff broke his M-1 rifle over one enemy's head, grabbed an *Arisaka* rifle from another's hands to bayonet him, and then shot a third mushroom-helmeted assailant. Wisely, the GIs made a fighting withdrawal, counting only two of their own dead and another missing. Such fierce local encounters would characterize the Item Pocket fighting lasting until April 25, and it was a company led by Captain Bernard Ryan that finally broke through the stubborn Item barrier.

On the twenty-fifth Ryan with two platoons climbed a key ridge and was savagely attacked by Japanese trying to drive them off. But they held, and then, assisted by other companies, began clearing the ridge to turn Item's seaward flank. Nevertheless resistance continued until April 28, when Highway 1 was finally opened to southbound American traffic. Now Griner's troops began to extend their grasp on the Urasoe-Mura Escarpment's western flank, suffering so severely that the division's losses rose above five hundred during a single day. By the morning of April 24, the western end of the Urasoe-Mura Escarpment was in American hands. Only Kakazu in Ushijima's outer defenses remained unconquered. Hoping to reduce that stubborn position, Hodge formed a special attack force under Brigadier General William Bradford, the Twenty-seventh's assistant division commander. Called "Bradford Force," it was to strike Kakazu early on the twenty-fourth. But that night during a heavy fog a powerful enemy artillery barrage struck the American forward elements. When Bradford Force attacked, its men found to their amazement that there was little or no resistance. Under cover of the fog and the bombardment, the wily Ushijima had ordered a general retreat to preserve his remaining strength.

For five days since April 19 the Japanese had fought a dogged defensive battle, limiting the Americans' gains to yards and at Kakazu stopping them in their tracks. But by darkness of April 23 the line had been pierced in so many places that it was in danger of collapsing with a consequent loss of many men; either by enemy action or suicide. So General Ushijima withdrew to his next chain of defenses.

In effect, the battle for southern Okinawa had advanced but a single, solid step—with many more steps to follow.

Kamikaze Bases Scourged/
Kikusui 4

CHAPTER SEVENTEEN

Major General Curtis Le May had been in command of the Twentieth Air Force since the summer of 1944. At thirty-nine, this burly flier, so big he could barely fit into a fighter cockpit, was anxious to apply his theories of incendiary bombing with the new B-29 Superfortress bomber then coming off the production lines. It was not until February 1945, however, that he had enough of these gigantic aircraft to stage a major firebombing raid—this time on Kobe and with such excellent results that an ecstatic Le May prepared for the monster March 9 strike at Tokyo that became the most destructive air raid in history.

Now believing—like all those "Bomber Barons" so detested by Dwight Eisenhower—that his command alone might bring Nippon to her knees, Le May was not happy to be ordered to concentrate on the enemy air bases on Kyushu in support of the Okinawa operation. From April 16 onward the Superforts hammered the *kamikaze* airfields, while their chief—speaking in language customarily garbled by the cigar or pipe clenched between his teeth—appealed to General H. H. "Hap" Arnold, chief of the U.S. Army Air Force, for permission to resume strategic bombing. It was not granted, if only because Fleet Admiral Nimitz had been able to convince the Joint Chiefs that the immediate short-range effects of punishing the suicider bases would in the long run prove more valuable than the long-range results of strategic bombing.

So the Superforts continued to strike the Kyushu fields, even though Admiral Ugaki frequently used all the late-model fighters at his disposal in an effort to destroy them. This was not quite possible, for his interceptors had neither the speed nor the fire-power necessary to take out a Superfort. Nevertheless, some vicious aerial duels developed high in the skies. One of the most fierce erupted on April 27 when a hundred B-29s attacked Kanoya and five other airfields. There were so many Japanese fighters aloft and buzzing the big bombers that Lieutenant Kenneth Hornbeck later told war correspondents: "The milk run is over—the cream is curdled." Lieutenant Philip Van Schuyler reported: "They must have made a hundred attacks on the eleven B-29s that I saw, and thirty on our four-plane section." One crippled Superfort flying out of formation was pounced on by four enemy fighters releasing white phosphorous bombs across its path. By skillful maneuver, the stricken aircraft broke clear. Four fighters fell and one Superfort was lost.

On the following day American gunners using their electronic computing gunsights claimed to have shot down thirty-six Japanese fighters together with thirteen "probables." Again, a B-29 was lost. Using the tactics of pattern-bombing, the Americans blanketed the Kyushu fields with fragmentation and demolition bombs, cratering runways and taxiways, riddling everything erect and destroying revetments. They also struck at hangars and shops filled with planes under repair while mangling irreplaceable tools. Japanese fighters compelled to land wherever they could on Kyushu became so scattered that Ugaki and Sugahara found it almost impossible to assemble them for concentrated flights intended to clear the Okinawa skies for the following *kamikaze*. Thus, many more suiciders than usual were exposed to the stuttering guns of naval and Marine flyers off the carriers, and more frequently the Marine Corsairs based at Yontan and Kadena.

Nevertheless, Ugaki and Sugahara managed to put together *Kikusui* 4, scheduled for two main attacks April 27 and 28, and a preliminary on April 22. Le May's attacks continued into May, and although a total of 24 Superforts were lost, with 233 damaged, the enemy's losses in fighters, though never known exactly, were certainly astronomical. Moreover, the Superforts achieved their objective in crippling the aerial fleets of Admiral Ugaki and General Sugahara.

As often happens, either because of luck, enemy indolence, or favorable weather, the "prelim" was more destructive than the "main bout." Twenty Navy and forty-six Army *kamikaze* came diving out of a haze concealing them from the gunners on the Hagushi ships. One crashed and sank a landing craft and another capsized the minesweeper *Swallow*. A third struck destroyer *Isherwood* among its depth charges aft, setting off a monster explosion that mangled the tin can's stern and sent it crawling slowly toward Kerama. Two other destroyers suffered minor damage. There might have been much more destruction at Hagushi but for the Marine pilots at Kadena and Yontan. They reported thirty-six kills, mostly among unskillful young suiciders unable to evade their attacks. Major George Axtell on his first combat mission over the Great Loo Choo became an ace in one flight, shooting down five Vals.

On April 27 and 28 the tireless Ugaki and Sugahara managed to put 100 *kamikaze* into the air. Four of them were *baka* bombers. On the first day they struck at dusk with fighter escort, inflicting only minor damage on four near-missed destroyers. But at 8:41 P.M. the hospital ship *Comfort* sailing southwest of Okinawa with a full load of patients on a clear night and during a full moon with the ship lighted according to the Geneva Convention—which by policy and preference the Japanese never observed—was deliberately dive-bombed by a *kamikaze*. The pilot was well aware of the privileged status of his target, having dived at it in a preliminary run, before pulling up and banking to dive again. His plane and bomb crashed through three superstructure decks before exploding in the surgery compartment.

Comfort did not sink, nor was there any panic. By a miracle of exemplary calm and the efforts of fire-fighting and repair crews, and despite casualties of thirty killed and thirty-three wounded—some of these either sick or wounded patients—the hospital ship was able to remain seaworthy while the repair crews dealt successfully with fire and flooding. Captain Adin Tooker took all precautions—swinging out undamaged lifeboats on weather decks and deliberately darkening his ship against the possible onslaught of another predatory *kamikaze*—and was thus able to make Guam in safety five days later.

The next day the B-29s—in vengeance it is to be hoped—scorched and scourged enemy fighters on Kyushu, leaving few escorts for the thirty-three suiciders bound for Task Group 58.4, one of two fast carrier groups still off Okinawa. Finding the Americans, two Zero suiciders dove out of the sun on destroyers *Haggard* and *Uhlmann*. By bad luck a 40 mm shell from *Uhlmann* hit *Haggard*'s main gun computer, leaving its five-inchers useless. Fortunately, both Zeros missed, but then another *kamikaze* crashed *Haggard*'s starboard side, detonating a 550-pound bomb against her forward engine. A second suicider missed *Haggard* by ten feet, but then as *Hazelwood* came to her assistance, a third scored a direct hit on her main deck that killed Commander Volckert Douw and forty-five officers and men. *Hazelwood* remained afloat but *Haggard* had to be towed to the Keramas.

Upon its arrival, *Haggard*'s skipper Lieutenant Commander Victor Soballe and all other hands on deck gaped in amazement and dismay at what they beheld in the anchorage. If not exactly a "graveyard of ships," it was at least a hospital emergency room stuffed with every category of floating cripple. Destroyers and all types of smaller ships—minesweepers, tenders, destroyer-escorts, LSMs, LCTs—in every stage of wreckage or disrepair were everywhere. Some had lost their masts, the smokestacks of others were either crumpled or missing, twisted guns hung over gunwales like broken teeth or were pointed uselessly upward, superstructures were caved in while in the sides of dozens of other vessels were gaping, jagged black holes—some of them covered by makeshift cofferdams looking like blisters—while missing bows were sometimes similarly protected against flooding or else had been jammed up against sagging bridges like steel accordions.

Commander Soballe's heart sank when he saw how many damaged vessels were in line for repairs ahead of his own. It could be weeks or more, and then, by the time *Haggard* would be ready to enter the floating dry dock, it might be discovered that she could not stand the flooding of just one more compartment and thus could not be repaired at all. So Soballe ordered his crew to turn to: to improvise and scrounge and cannibalize and invent and "borrow" (that universal service euphemism for pilferage or "pinching") whatever they needed but could not obtain by requisition. This required not only skill-fingered sailors but light-fingered ones. There were enough of the first kind among *Haggard*'s welders, electricians, steamfitters, carpenters, and the other technical "mates" needed to run a modern warship, and a superabundance of the second kind among bos'n's mates and ordinary deckhands. The light-fingered details scrounged or borrowed enough scraps and pieces of lumber and other materials needed to patch a hole twenty by eighteen feet where the suicider had crashed. Another hole through which seawater had flowed to flood engine and boiler rooms was plugged when Soballe and others put on diving equipment to cover it with a seven-ton temporary patch, after which the rooms were pumped out. Meanwhile, the black gang ingeniously rebuilt an after boiler from fragments of a wrecked one, using whatever scraps that would fit to repair steam lines to the engines. So resurrected, lighting off one boiler, the crew got their beloved ship under way, and in four months sailed her halfway around the world to the Norfolk Navy Yard.

The ups and downs of the air war in Okinawa are shown here: a P-47, broken and burning after crashing during takeoff; and grinning, cigar-smoking pilots from the Second Marine fighter patrol after they had shot down fifteen enemy bombers operating off Yontan Airfield.

ABOVE: Ancestor-worshiping Okinawans usually buried their dead in huge lyre-shaped tombs, which the Japanese later fortified and the Americans overran using tactics of "corkscrew and blowtorch"—explosive and flame, either aimed or dropped. Here a typical tomb serves as cover for a battalion command post.

BELOW: A phosphorous grenade explodes in a shattered building as Yanks attempt to dislodge a sniper hidden in the ruins.

The Japanese hunkered down tenaciously in caves forming the "Little Siegfried Line" as Army infantrymen and Marines battled close in and also sought the help of tanks (BELOW). It was a bitter struggle for the capital city of Naha.

En route to Okinawa, Ernie Pyle, the most beloved correspondent of World War II, was serenaded by an accordion-playing Marine.

Here is Ernie Pyle waiting beside a jeep on a road in tiny Ie Shima, an island northwest of Okinawa. Moments later he was killed by a Japanese sniper.

Pyle was buried on Ie Shima, an Army chaplain offering the benediction as the doughboys Pyle loved looked on.

BELOW: Later on strategic Ie Shima, airstrips were being built to send P-47s on their way to Japan.

Late in June, American forces could ease up. The Japanese had finally been overwhelmed. Here, Leathernecks and GIs were able to rest from their battles. One soldier took over a bomb-shelter cave and made it his home.

Toward the end of the fighting on Okinawa, there occurred the astonishing phenomenon of Japanese soldiers surrendering en masse, rather than killing themselves, as was customary. Here are hundreds of the 10,000 who laid down their arms, guarded by a lone American GI.

American soldiers who overran the cliff where Lieutenant General Mitsuru Ushijima, commander of the Japanese troops on Okinawa, committed suicide, along with his chief of staff, Lieutenant General Isamu Cho, found no trace of their bodies but only General Ushijima's dress blouse. Okinawa was finally secured.

Last Gasp of the
Samurai Cho

On April 29, Emperor Hirohito's birthday and the most important holiday in Japan, Lieutenant General Mitsuru Ushijima sum-
moned his top commanders to his headquarters in a tunnel
underneath Shuri Castle. For days they had been privately argu-
ing over Isamu Cho's proposal for a massive counter-stroke
against the Americans. Now Ushijima wished them to discuss
whether or not his strategy for defending Okinawa should be
changed. Some historians say Ushijima was not present, others
insist that he was. It does not seem likely, however, that the
Thirty-second Army commander—even though it was not his
custom to attend staff discussions—would ignore such a momen-
tous meeting called by himself.

Ushijima's chiefs sat on canvas camp chairs at a rough flat
table covered with maps. Around them the stones of the tunnel
glistened with sweat. Water from the moat surrounding medieval
Shuri seeped through crevices in the wall or dripped incessantly
on the floor of beaten earth. Dim light glinted weakly off the
glasses worn by most of the officers in attendance or winked on
the stars of the numerous generals present.

Isamu Cho sat close to Ushijima, staring arrogantly into the questioning gaze of his arch rival, Colonel Hiromichi Yahara. Just as he had predicted the debacle of General Cho's abortive counter-attack of April 12–13, the rigidly rational Yahara was now prepared to oppose what he knew would be a plan for an even greater and more disastrous counter-stroke. By his patrician bearing he made it clear that he could not be bullied by either the rank or the fiery rhetoric of the burly general now rising to address the meeting.

Cho began with an incredible untruth: that the Japanese soldier—in the main from four to six inches shorter than his American enemies and from thirty to fifty pounds lighter—was a superb hand-to-hand fighter who could easily overpower the soft, effete American devils. A general clearing of throats and grunts of approval followed this absurd remark, either born of the School of the Rosy Report or emanating from the *sake* bottles being passed freely around. Very quickly most of the commanders present supported Cho's plan: Lieutenant General Takeo Fujioka, commander of the Sixty-second Division, and also the plan's coauthor; Lieutenant General Tatsumi Amamiya, swallowing his detestation of the boastful Fujioka in his eagerness to lead his untested Twenty-fourth Division into battle at last; and Major General Kosuke Wada, chief of the Fifth Artillery Command. Wada agreed with the others that the Thirty-second Army had made an achievement unprecedented in Pacific warfare: it had preserved its main body intact after a month of fighting.

This, Yahara bluntly interjected, happened only because the Americans had not yet hurled their full strength against the Naha-Shuri-Yonabaru line. But now that the outer defenses had fallen, because of the April 12–13 fiasco, the American commander was strengthening his assault forces, according to intelligence reports. An even bigger disaster would ensue if Cho's massive counter-offensive were approved, he warned. And to speak of the valor of the troops was foolish, because even now, since there had been no issue of sweet-potato brandy on the emperor's birthday, the men were discontented. For thirty days these gallant men had risen every morning to look down upon a Hagushi Anchorage still choked with enemy ships. The Divine Winds had not blown them away. It was difficult for even Japanese soldiers to believe that the Navy would come to their rescue—nor could they be blamed for complaining about being asked to fight alone one day's sail from the homeland.

It was true, Isamu Cho replied slowly, that the Americans had not thrown in all their strength. But they were doing so now. There was a new Marine division in the enemy's assault line, the First, the hated butchers of Guadalcanal. Another—the Sixth—was due to join them. This was the moment to destroy the Americans' fresh power. But, Cho continued, the Thirty-second Army had also been reinforced. Had not our chief General Ushijima in his wisdom concluded that the enemy was not interested in storming the Minatoga Beaches, and so had ordered our comrades of the Twenty-fourth Division and Forty-fourth Brigade to join us here? Now it is *we* who are at full strength. Let us strike the enemy immediately and annihilate them before they can grind down to our main line.

Careful, full-scale counter-attack, not the foolish glory of the Banzai, would crush the Americans. There must be help from the *kamikaze*, then massed artillery fire with the troops attacking all along the line. The fresh Twenty-fourth Division would be hurled at the center and open a hole through which the Forty-fourth Brigade would pour in a thrust to the west coast. The Forty-fourth would then wheel south and the First Marine Division would be isolated and annihilated. The American Twenty-fourth Corps would be rolled up. There should also be counter-landings on both flanks. The Twenty-sixth Shipping Engineer Regiment would embark from Naha in barges, small boats, and native canoes to strike the rear of the Marine division. Later, the youths of the Twenty-sixth, Twenty-eighth, and Twenty-ninth Sea Raiding Squadrons would cross the reef and wade ashore to help the engineers. A similar counter-landing would strike the rear of the Seventh Infantry Division on the east.

It would be difficult to conceive a more complicated plan of attack, and Cho's proposal calling for so many disconnected and disparate sallies—a montage of uncoordinated sorties if ever there was one—paid absolutely no heed to what the enemy's reaction might be. Moreover, it was made doubly difficult by the Japanese unfailing reliance on a night attack to cancel out the American superiority in artillery, even if this meant confusing their own troops. Yet, when Colonel Yahara arose to criticize the operation, he praised it as tactically excellent, probably because he was about to demolish it as a strategic monstrosity and did not want to alienate Cho entirely. Yahara said:

"To take the offensive with inferior forces against absolutely superior enemy forces is reckless and will only lead to certain defeat. We must continue the current operation, calmly recognizing its final destiny—for annihilation is inevitable no matter what is done—and maintain to the bitter end the principle of a strategic holding action. If we should fail, the period of maintaining a strategic holding action, as well as the holding action for the decisive battle for the homeland, will be shortened. Moreover, our forces will inflict but small losses on the enemy, while on the other hand, scores of thousands of our troops will have been sacrificed in vain as victims of the offensive."

Yahara sat down.

It was now up to Ushijima.

He nodded to Cho.

The attack would begin at dawn on May 4. Before that, the flank counter-landings would be launched. Before them the artillery would commence, and before everything would come the *kamikaze*.

The Japanese aerial assaults began at six o'clock on the night of May 3. Once again, the bombers sought to get at the rich pickings in the Hagushi Anchorage, but thirty-six of them were shot down and the rest forced to unload at high altitude, with little damage. Only the suicide-diving *kamikaze* broke through. They sank destroyer *Little* and an LSM, while damaging two mine layers and an LCS. After midnight, sixty bombers struck Tenth Army rear areas, coming in scattering window. Terrible antiaircraft fire rose in crisscrossing streams of light, as though a million narrow-beamed searchlights were aimed into the night, and the bombers dropped their loads aimlessly—though some of them landed in a Marine evacuation hospital.

An hour later Marine amtanks guarding Machinato Airfield on the west coast fired at voices on the beach. American cruisers, destroyers, and gunboats on "flycatcher" patrol shot at squat Japanese barges sliding darkly upcoast from Naha. The barges lost their way. Instead of landing far enough north to take the Marines in their rear, they veered inshore and blundered into the outposts of B Company, First Marines.

The Japanese sent up a screeching and gobbling of battle cries and the surprised Marines sprang to their guns. All up and down the sea wall the battle raged, with Marine amtracks moving out to sea and coming in again to grind the Japs to pieces between two fires. Some five hundred Japanese died in this futile west-flank landing.

The east-flank landings came to the same annihilating end. Navy patrol boats sighted the Japanese craft. They fired at them and turned night into day with star-shells. Soldiers of the Seventh Division's Reconnaissance Troops joined the sailors to complete the destruction of four hundred men.

At dawn, the main attack began.

It went straight to the doom that Colonel Yahara had pre-dicted. Wave after wave of the Twenty-fourth Division's men shuffled forward to death in that gray dawn, moving among their own artillery shells, taking this risk in hopes of getting in on the Americans. But the soldiers of the Seventh and Seventy-seventh Divisions held firm—while American warships, sixteen battalions of division artillery, and twelve battalions of heavier corps artil-lery, plus 134 airplanes, smothered the enemy in a wrathful blanket of steel and explosive. Ships as big as the fourteen-inch-gunned *New York* and *Colorado,* as small as gunboats with 20 mm cannons, ranged up and down the east coast firing at the Japanese on call.

Across the island, the *kamikaze* dove again on ships in the Hagushi Anchorage, again falling on the luckless small vessels of the radar picket screen. With them were the *baka* bombs. This May 4 one of the *baka* hit the light mine-layer *Shea* and set it temporarily on fire. The *kamikaze* also sank two more destroyers, *Luce* and *Morrison,* as well as two LSMs, while damaging the car-rier *Sangamon,* the cruiser *Birmingham,* another pair of destroyers, a minesweeper, and an LCS. Again, they failed to get at the cargo and transport ships. And they lost 95 planes.

Ashore, Isamu Cho's massive counterthrust was being broken by that material power for which Mitsuru Ushijima had shown such profound respect. Much of the Japanese assault died aborn-ing. Sometimes the Japanese closed, but rarely. There were see-saw battles up and down some of the ridges held by the Seventy-seventh, but they ended with the GIs either in command of their previous position or holding new ground farther inside the Japanese territory. One battalion of the Japanese Twenty-fourth Division got behind the Seventy-seventh on the left, but it was annihilated by a reserve battalion of the Seventh Division in a three-day fight. Otherwise the Twenty-fourth Division never punched that hole through which the Forty-fourth Brigade was to race and isolate the First Marine Division.

And the First began attacking on the morning of May 4. Even as the GIs on their left bore the brunt of Cho's big sally, these Marines were battling southeast toward the key bastion of Shuri. They scored gains of up to four hundred yards. The next day they attacked again, once more pushing the Japanese back—even though their advance was made more costly by the fact that they were up against rested battalions of the Japanese Sixty-second Division. By the night of May 5 the Marines had picked up another three hundred yards. By that time Lieutenant General Isamu Cho's massive stroke had been completely shattered. Those two days of fighting had cost the Japanese 6,227 dead. The Seventh and Seventy-seventh Divisions had lost 714 men killed or wounded while holding the line, the First Marine Division had taken losses of 649 men in the more costly business of attack. The next day the First gained another three hundred yards, and added a fourth Medal of Honor winner to its rolls since coming into the line on May 1. That day Corporal John Fardy smothered a grenade with his life, as had Pfc. William Foster. Sergeant Elbert Kinser did it on May 4. Two days before that, Corpsman Robert Bush had risked his life to give plasma to a wounded officer, driving off a Japanese rush with pistol and carbine, killing six of the enemy and refusing evacuation though badly wounded.

There would be more Medals of Honor won in the days to come. The First Division by May 5 had come against Ushijima's main line, as had the GIs on their left. In front of the First was the western half of the Shuri bastion. To their right was Naha, and this would be assigned to the Sixth Marine Division the next day. In the sector of both these Marine divisions were systems of interlocking fortified ridges such as those encountered on Iwo Jima. Nor would the way be made easy here by further counterattack.

A change had taken place at Shuri Castle. In tears, Lieutenant General Ushijima had promised Colonel Yahara that from now

on he would listen to no one but him. The Ushijima-Cho relationship had ended in the recrimination of a red and useless defeat. Isamu Cho argued no longer. He became silent and stoical,
convinced now that only time stood between the Thirty-second
Army and ultimate destruction.

Minatoga:
A Missed Opportunity

CHAPTER NINETEEN

One of the still-unexplained puzzlers of the Battle for Okinawa is why Lieutenant General Simon Bolivar Buckner allowed two veteran Marine divisions to stand idle in the north—the First for a month, the Sixth for nearly two weeks—instead of using them to relieve one or two Army infantry divisions badly battered in his three-division assault on the Naha-Shuri-Yonabaru line. The answer, unpleasant though this speculation may be, seems to be that Buckner wanted the Army infantry to have the honor of crushing the Japanese Thirty-second Army.

There is nothing especially biased or prejudiced in such an attitude, and it is actually much more common among commanders of rival services than is generally understood. A similar decision by a Marine general occurred when Major General William Rupertus, commanding the First Marine Division at Peleliu, hesitated much too long before relieving his crippled First Regiment with a regiment from the Eighty-first Infantry Division. He did it only after ordered to do so by Major General Roy Geiger, who was commander of the Third Marine Amphibious Corps. But Buckner's reluctance was somewhat more surprising in that the First Marine Division was probably the most experienced fighting formation in the American Armed Forces; 70 percent of the Sixth—though new to battle as a unit—was composed of veterans from other divisions in other campaigns.

It was not until April 28 that Buckner decided to put fresh troops into his renewed down-island offensive. The Seventh would remain in place on the left, and the Ninety-sixth would be relieved by the Seventy-seventh. The First Marine Division would relieve the Twenty-seventh Infantry Division on the Seventy-seventh's right with the Sixth Marine Division holding the western flank. Thus the line, Seventh, Seventy-seventh, First, Sixth: Twenty-fourth Corps, Third Corps.

Almost simultaneously with this realignment there arose a dispute over a proposal made by Major General Andrew Bruce of the Seventy-seventh. Just before Cho's counter-attack, Bruce had suggested that his division envelop Ushijima's rear by storming the Minatoga Beaches below him. On Leyte, Bruce's Seventy-seventh had made a strikingly successful landing behind the Japanese line at Ormoc—where "the 77th rolled a pair of sevens"— and he was confident he could do the same on Okinawa. Once ashore, his division could either move inland to take Iwa, a road and communications center on the island's southern tip, or push north to join the Seventh near Yonabaru.

Buckner gave no serious consideration to the suggestion after his supply officer, Brigadier General David Blakelock, reported that though he could supply food for the operation, Tenth Army had not enough ammunition to spare for it. On the last count, Blakelock's analysis was correct; for even Tenth Army's splendid service of supply had not yet been able to compensate for the loss of those two ammunition ships on April 6. Buckner was also aware that Tenth Army planners had rejected the Minatoga Beaches before L-day: the reefs were too dangerous, the beaches inadequate, and the area exposed to strong enemy counter-attack.

Beach outlets also were commanded by a plateau, and Bruce's landing would be too far south to receive support from Hodge's corps in the north and was also out of range of his artillery.

These were indeed daunting considerations, although hardly more formidable than the drying reef and seawall at Tarawa or even the reefs and seawall at Hagushi. Other division chiefs besides Bruce supported his proposal, although not necessarily to be executed by his division. Major General Pedro del Valle of the First Marine Division believed a Minatoga landing was advisable, although it should be made by the more experienced Second Marine Division, still in Third Corps reserve. Major General Lemuel Shepherd of the Sixth said later he had suggested use of the Second several times to Buckner, pointing out that the logistics argument did not apply to this formation because it had enough beans and bullets of its own to sustain a thirty-day assault. A landing by the Second, he wrote later, "would have seriously threatened Ushijima's rear and required him to withdraw troops from the Shuri battle or employ his limited reserve to contain the landing."

Army historians of Okinawa in their book on the campaign were agreed that Minatoga would have produced logistical difficulties and might have failed, *but only if it were attempted before the end of April.* If made after May 5—the date that Cho's abortive counter-strike was shattered—it could not have been opposed by more than two or three thousand men. Colonel John Guerard, Tenth Army operations officer, had learned by late April of Ushijima's order for the Japanese Twenty-fourth Division and Forty-fourth Brigade to move north into Shuri, where they joined Cho's assault. This left Minatoga lightly defended, and Guerard, who had originally opposed a landing there, now strongly recommended it. So did General Hodge, who went to Tenth Army headquarters to urge Buckner to envelop the enemy there. But the Tenth Army commander did not agree, again basing his re-

jection on the logistics argument even though he now knew that
the Second Marine Division could operate for a month on its
own supplies.

Buckner's decision became highly controversial in the stateside press even before the Okinawa campaign had ended. Such
influential newspapers as the Washington *Star* and the New York
Herald-Tribune, probably at the urging of Admiral King, flatly
stated that the secondary landing should have been made. Some
historians in defense of Buckner have suggested that if the Tenth
Army commander had even suspected that the Okinawa fighting
would continue through May, and then for almost another agonizing month in June, he might have preferred to risk a quick
end to it by landing in Ushijima's rear. This is a specious argument, the purest conjecture apparently based upon nothing more
substantial than a desire to exonerate the Tenth Army commander for having failed to take what can only be described as a
gamble with little risk. All the odds after May 5 were in Buckner's
favor: an inferior foe defending against his own superiority in the
number and quality of his troops, as well as in supply and in
control of the air above and sea surrounding Okinawa.

Caught between four American divisions to his front, with
another in reserve and a garrison division also available behind
them; and in his rear a seventh veteran division; pounded from
land, sea, and sky; hopelessly isolated and cut off from reinforce-
ment or supplies, with the *kikusui* attacks of no help on land,
Ushijima's Thirty-second Army could either be starved into submission or—if surrender was still so unthinkable to *Samurai* such
as Ushijima, Cho, and Yahara—compelled to make a final "glorious" sally that would be broken in blood ending in mass suicide.

Meanwhile, with the Minatoga opportunity rejected as un-
feasible, General Buckner still had to face the growing and open
disenchantment of Admirals Spruance and Turner with the slow
progress of Tenth Army on land. Turner had repeatedly urged
on Buckner the necessity for a quick conquest to relieve the ter-

rible pressure of the *kikusui* on the concentration of American ships off Okinawa. For such a huge body of vessels to remain so long as plainly visible targets of a suicidal enemy was indeed unprecedented in military history. This, of course, was not entirely the fault of General Buckner but rather enemy policy—in a sense—to "bleed all over" the Americans and thus drown them in Japanese blood. Again, this was small comfort to either Spruance or Turner. Buckner's reply to the Expeditionary Force commander was that he was moving slowly in an effort to "save lives." To Admiral Spruance this was not a convincing argument, for he wrote: "I doubt if the Army's slow, methodical method of fighting really saves any lives in the long run. It merely spreads the casualties over a longer period. The longer period greatly increases the naval casualties when Jap air attacks on ships is a continuing factor . . . There are times when I get impatient for some of Holland ('Howlin' Mad') Smith's drive."

Spruance was right: lives are definitely not "saved" by a carefully slow assault, they are merely spread out in time, but in the end the number of casualties is the same or almost so. If an assaulting unit comes to, say, an enemy .47 antitank position protected by machine guns, thus making it impossible for supporting tanks to advance, and decides to call for artillery to knock it out before attacking, in the subsequent assault it will almost certainly discover that shells simply cannot pulverize strong and clever defenses. Foot soldiers will still have to go in there with hand weapons, with flamethrowers, grenades, and satchel charges, and the time lost waiting for artillery to destroy the position will have been wasted. And their casualties will be the same as if they had attacked instantly.

Even General Buckner himself on May 1 had acknowledged at a press conference that Okinawa would fall only to tactics he described as "corkscrew and blowtorch": the corkscrew being explosives and the blowtorch flamethrowers and napalm. But all of these have to be *aimed!* Aimed close up. Visible. They cannot be

fired from a mile or more to the rear in an arc, which would be
like skipping stones on water. Because every defensive position
has a mouth or aperture through which its weapon can be fired,
bullets, grenades, satchel charges, or flame have to be hurled,
thrown, or squirted through these openings. Again, close up.
Even napalm will skid, and because it is always dropped from an
airplane, it has about as much chance to enter a foot-by-foot or
even a two feet–by–two feet opening as has a camel "to pass
through the eye of a needle."

Go ahead, ask the question, "What's the difference—slow or
speedy—if the results are the same?" The answer is that the time
lost will extend the exposure of a supporting fleet such as Spruance's to the assaults of the *kikusui*, and also delay the departure
of such naval forces to participate in another amphibious invasion
elsewhere or release the fast carriers to strike homeland Japan.
Finally, slow, careful land assaults could delay the entire Pacific
timetable to the great pleasure of the enemy, for the one thing
Japan could not afford to waste in the spring of 1945 was time.

Spruance and Turner could not forget what had happened to
the escort carrier *Liscome Bay* at Makin, when sixty-five hundred
GIs moving slowly took a week to conquer a weak position in an
operation that should have been finished in hours. Ordinarily,
Liscome Bay would have been long gone from the impact area, but
the ship was sunk on the last day by an enemy submarine, with
extensive loss of life. Similarly, because of slow progress on Okinawa, ships and many seamen and seagoing Marines were being
lost daily on the Hagushi Anchorage.

The admirals were also anguished by and ever mindful of the
ordeal of their men, these unsung heroes, aboard those exposed
ships, especially those of the Radar Picket Line scourged by hundreds of *kamikaze* and *baka*. Men were horribly burned. They
were blown into the ocean, either to drown or pass agonizing
hours awaiting rescue and the ministrations of medical corpsmen.
Those who survived the suiciders' screaming dives went for days

on end without sleep, their nerves exposed and quivering like wires stripped of insulation. Lying wide-eyed on their bunks, they waited to hear the dreaded telltale click and static of the ship's bullhorns being activated—like a starter's gun sending them leaping erect and running so that they were already in motion when the shrill, strident notes of "General Quarters" burst in their ears.

Men in the boiler rooms worked in intense heat. The superheaters, built to give the quick pressure needed for sudden high-speed maneuvering under aerial attack, were often kept running three or four days at a time, though they had been made for intermittent use. But it had to be that way, for war off Okinawa was war at a moment's notice. Very little time separated that moment when radar screens became clouded with pips of approaching "bogies" and the shrieking suiciders came plunging to the attack. An attempt to give the crews more warning of enemy approach had to be abandoned, one war correspondent reported: "The strain of waiting, the anticipated terror, made vivid from past experience, sent some men into hysteria, insanity, breakdown."

Similar reports reaching Admiral Nimitz led him to request from MacArthur the return of most of the ships of the Seventh Fleet he had so generously loaned the Southwest Pacific chief at the start of the Leyte campaign. He wanted to relieve some of Spruance's ships. But MacArthur had already protected himself against compliance with this agreed-upon condition by deliberately committing these vessels—as well as the Eleventh Air Force and the Eighth Army—to a useless campaign in the southern Philippines in order to prevent their scheduled transfer to Nimitz. Such tactics, of course, were nothing new in World War II. During the Battle of the Bulge General George Patton deliberately committed his beloved Fourth Armored Division to an unnecessary battle to prevent its being taken from him by General Omar Bradley, who had already commandeered his Tenth Armored Division. But MacArthur's move was the soul of ingratitude for

Nimitz's generosity. And it was compounded by the general's return to his old, discredited theme of "minimal losses" by com-
paring the ease and low casualties of his southern Philippine
campaign—again against mud-and-logs and fragmented troops—
to Tenth Army's higher losses moving through steel-concrete-
and-coral defenses manned by soldiers determined to fight to the
death. Because of this typical MacArthurian selfishness, the
scourging of the Fifth Fleet continued.

In fairness to Buckner, the defensive complex into which he
was plunging straight ahead could not be reduced in any other
way than corkscrew and blowtorch. But the attack could have
been more impetuous and spirited, less dependent on what General William Westmoreland in Vietnam a generation later exco-
riated as "the firebase psychosis": i.e., a tendency to stop at every
obstacle and call for artillery. But it also must not be forgotten
that Buckner summarily rejected the one opportunity for maneuver on Okinawa: the envelopment of Ushijima's rear by a landing
at Minatoga. *Why*, will never be known, for this able, considerate,
and dedicated soldier did not live long enough to write his mem-
oirs or at least an explanation of his position.

But was the straight-ahead, annihilating attack the only so-
lution to the destruction of Ushijima's remaining sixty thousand
men? Tenth Army had already secured and improved all the air
and port facilities on Okinawa. For the Japanese, there was no
way out, around, under, over, or through. Did no one suggest
cutting off the enemy to let him starve? Why not emulate Nimitz's "island-hopping" strategy in the Pacific, leaving enemy gar-
risons to "wither on the vine" by seizing the biggest and most
useful islands while neutralizing those lying in between by aerial
bombing. The Japanese could have been whittled and demoralized by constant aerial, land, and sea bombardment—even goaded
into those desperation, back-breaking Banzai attacks so attractive
to the *Samurai* character. Doubtless, they would not remain completely contained but would sally forth in typical night forays

aimed at spreading terror and destruction. But this could have only minor success. It could never have inflicted casualties among the Americans comparable to what they suffered in Buckner's final straight-ahead assault.

Nevertheless, perhaps because of the importunate appeals of Spruance and Turner—who, after all, were his superior officers —General Buckner did quickly schedule another grand offensive for May 11. The Ninety-sixth Division back on line would be on the eastern (or left) flank, the Seventy-seventh on its right; next, First Marine Division, and then the Sixth on the right, or western, flank. General Hodge would command his Twenty-fourth Corps troops on the left and would be the tactical commander of the entire front, with Geiger leading the Third Corps Marines. It was typical of Geiger, whose courtesy matched Buckner's, that he did not protest the selection of Hodge as tactical chief, even though he was his senior and about to receive his third star.

This offensive was to be a continuation of the others with the same tactics, including the capable General Bruce's innovation of concentrating on a limited objective from which fire could be brought to bear on the enemy's reverse slope. Just before the jump-off date, however, the Great Loo Choo's gray, growling, and moisture-laden sky became the Lord of the Battlefield.

May: Rain, Mud, Blood—
and Breakthrough!

CHAPTER TWENTY

On May 7 the skies of the Great Loo Choo opened with prolonged and torrential rains that reminded First Division Leathernecks of the month-long monsoon they had endured in the
New Britain campaign. During seventeen days of intermittent
storms, some fifteen inches of rain fell on Okinawa.

Nothing could stand against it; a letter from home in the
sodden pocket of a GI or Marine had to be read and re-read and
memorized before the ink ran and it fell apart in less than a week;
a pair of socks lasted no longer; and a pack of cigarettes became
watery and uninflammable unless smoked the same day, or else,
along with matches, they were kept dry within a contraceptive
inside a helmet liner. Pocketknife blades rusted together, and
watches recorded the period of their own decay. Rain made gar-
bage of the food; pencils swelled into useless pulp; fountain pens
became clogged with watery ink, and their points burst apart; rifle
barrels turned blue with mold and had to be slung upside down
to keep the raindrops from fouling their bores. Sometimes bullets
in the rifle magazines stuck together, while machine gunners had
to go over their belts daily, extracting the bullets and oiling them

to prevent their sticking to the cloth loops. Everything lay damp and sodden, squishy and squashy to the touch, exuding a steady and musty reek that was the odor of decaying vegetation.

To the Americans out in the open—unlike their enemies warm, dry, and snug in their underground warrens—there were only three things of value to be found in this gurgling, gushing, rushing, streaming, dripping, drenching downpour that turned Okinawa's numerous narrow and shallow streams into raging, boiling, white torrents of water: a dry place, hot and solid food, and most of all—most unbelievably important of all!—a hot cup of coffee. At sundown before blackout discipline would be in force, among squads huddling together all over the island, tiny fires were made of the wrappings of cigarette packages and the waxed covers of K rations, and water heated in a canteen cup containing grains of K ration soluble coffee—thus were their bellies fortified against another cold black rainy night.

And the rain on Okinawa made Okinawa mud. It was unique because it was everywhere: in the ears, under the nails, inside leggings, or squeezed coarse and cold between the toes. It got into a man's weapons, it was in his food, and sometimes he could feel it grinding like emery grains between his teeth. Whatever was slotted, pierced, open, or empty received this mud. Wounds also. Men prayed not to get hit while rain fell and made mud. It embarrassed drivers of bulldozers and made pick-and-shovel coolies of those lordly tank troops. Some days it denied Americans the use of roads altogether, and GIs and Marines on the attack again often had to be supplied by airdrop. Frequently it was hardly possible to walk in it. A few strides and a man's shoes were coated and heavy with mud. Two more and they seemed as though encased in lead. A third step and it was easier to slip out of them before the mud sucked them off and walk in it barefooted. Engineers on the airfields actually put their shoes aside and worked in sacking drawn over their feet and tied around the knees.

It was this mud in which the entire Tenth Army lay immobilized on the eighth of May, the day on which smeared and dripping Marines and GIs received the splendid news that Germany had surrendered.

"So what?" they snorted in contempt.

The death of Hitler and the destruction of his Third Reich meant about as much to these embattled Americans as the pardon of one condemned criminal might mean to another still under sentence of death. General Ushijima and the stubborn soldiers of his Thirty-second Army were their only concern, and at that very moment Ushijima was taking advantage of the rain that had stalled his enemy to strengthen his flanks while his artillerists reminded their foe that the air still sang and shrieked with invisible death. Ushijima also reinforced the strongpoints guarding the vital forty-foot-wide east-west highway behind his barrier line, settling down to that grim step-for-step war of attrition urged on him by Colonel Yahara. Because of these defenses—and the incessant rain—the Tenth Army drive southward on May 9 moved even slower.

At the same time, the *kikusui* scourging of the invasion fleet rose to a crescendo of fury. Opposing them were those Marine Corsair pilots from Yontan and Kadena who had come to the Great Loo Choo expecting to fly close-up support of the ground Leathernecks, only to be called to the rescue of the radar picket ships. They rode the suiciders down to unintended destruction away from their target vessels, sometimes even after the American pilots had expended all their ammunition. A few of them attacked the *kamikaze* and *baka* with their whirling propellers, just as Lieutenant Robert Klingman did in the bizarre Battle of the Frozen Guns.

That was the dogfight fought at over 40,000 feet among a Japanese two-seater Nick fighter and two Corsairs piloted by Klingman and Captain Kenneth Reusser. On combat air patrol over Ie Shima on May 10 they spotted the vapor trail of the

Japanese at 25,000 feet. They chased him, climbing steadily from 10,000 altitude until, after a pursuit of 185 miles, firing off most of their ammunition to lighten their load, they caught up with the Nick at 38,000 feet.

They closed.

Reusser shot up all his ammunition in damaging the Japanese's left wing and left engine. Klingman bored in to within 50 feet and pressed his gun button. His guns were frozen. He drove in, his propellers whirling. They chopped up the enemy's rudder and left it dangling. In the Nick's rear cockpit the gunner was banging his fists on his own frozen guns. The Corsair's big propellers chewed on. Klingman turned and came back for another pass. He cut off the rudder and loosened the right stabilizer. He was running out of gas. He decided he didn't have enough to make Okinawa anyway and turned for a third pass. He cut off the Nick's stabilizer. The plane went into a spin, and at 15,000 feet it lost both wings and plunged into the East China Sea.

Klingman started down, losing his oxygen at 18,000 feet, and his power at 10,000. But he landed at Kadena Field, dead-stick and on his belly, his wings and fuselage sewn with bullet holes and pieces of the destroyed Nick in his cowling.

Nevertheless, the losses inflicted on the enemy aircraft did not dissuade Admiral Turner from asking Buckner once again to speed up his attack, and the Tenth Army chief obliged by scheduling a massive, four-division assault for May 11.

The Tenth Army had four full divisions abreast. General Hodge's Twenty-fourth Corps was on the left (or east) with the Ninety-sixth and Seventy-seventh divisions in that order, and General Geiger's Third Corps on the right (or west) with the First and Sixth. The Ninety-sixth's objective was Conical Hill, the Seventy-seventh would buck at Shuri Castle, the First strike the Dakeshi-Wana-Wana complex guarding Shuri, and the Sixth at Sugar Loaf Hill. Of these four objectives, those facing the Marine divisions were the strongest.

Sugar Loaf opposite the Sixth was at least the formidable equal of the bloody meat grinder of Iwo Jima. It was not just one hill but a complex of three. Sugar Loaf itself did not look difficult, just an oblong ridge about fifty feet high. But it was protected to its left rear by the Half-Moon and on its right rear by the Horseshoe, a long ridge bristling with mortars. On the left where the First Division was attacking was Shuri Heights, also stuffed with gunners who could hit the Sixth on Sugar Loaf as well as the First to their front.

To attempt to get at Sugar Loaf was to be hit by the others. To strike at the others was to be hit by Sugar Loaf. But this was not suspected until the main position was reached on the morning of May 14, after a fighting crossing of the Asa River and steady grinding down of smaller hills guarding the approaches.

On that May 14 most of the morning was spent evacuating Marines stricken while crossing the flat open ground approaching that harmless-looking loaf of earth. In the afternoon a charge with supporting tanks was driven back when three of four tanks were knocked out, and artillery from Sugar's front, left-rear, and rear fell among the riflemen. A second assault before dusk reached Sugar Loaf's base. But of 150 Marines from the Second Battalion, Twenty-second, who began it, only 40 reached the hill. They were exhausted. They were out of supplies. It was getting dusk. Suddenly, the enemy stopped firing. The men realized that someone was speaking to them. It was Major Henry Courtney, the battalion's executive officer.

"If we don't take the top of this hill tonight," he was saying, "the Japs will be down here to drive us away in the morning. The only way we can take it is to make a Banzai charge of our own. I'm asking for volunteers."

There was hardly a pause before the Glory Kid stepped forward, grinning.

"I hate to sound like a guy in a dime novel," said Corporal Rusty Golar, "but what the hell did we come here for?"

There were 19 other volunteers from this exhausted remnant, and 26 fresh men who appeared carrying supplies. Major Courtney took these 45 Marines up Sugar Loaf under cover of darkness, heaving grenades as they went, digging in under the protection of their own mortars. From the Horseshoe and Half-Moon came machine-gun fire and mortar shells, while grenades came up at them from the reverse slope of Sugar Loaf. At midnight, Courtney heard the enemy gathering below. He decided to strike them.

"Take all the grenades you can carry," he whispered. "When we get over the top, throw them and start digging in."

They went out, behind Courtney. They heard the major shout, "Keep coming, there's a mess of them down there!" And then they heard the explosion of the mortar shell that killed him. They answered with grenades of their own, hanging on to Sugar Loaf while all of the Japanese positions struck at them, while a cold rain swept in from the East China Sea, until the mists of the morning showed that there were only 20 men left of the 45 who had come up the night before.

In that mist Rusty Golar, the self-styled Storybook Marine, fought the battle he had always sought. With his buddies he was on the right flank of Sugar Loaf, where he set up his light machine gun. With daylight, the Japanese on Horseshoe Hill to his right opened up on him. Golar fired back. The Japanese on Half-Moon to the left opened up. With a deep, booming "Yeah!" Golar swiveled his gun to rake Half-Moon.

Back and forth it went, the whipsawing Japanese fire, the booming "Yeah!" of the Glory Kid and his own alternating bursts. It went on while Sugar Loaf's defenders were gradually whittled to a handful, while men trying to bring up ammunition were killed or wounded, continuing until only Golar and a few others were left alive. By then the Glory Kid's machine-gun belts had all been fired. He drew his pistol, yelling, "Gotta use what I got left!" He emptied it twice more. He threw it at the caves below and began scurrying about the hillcrest to gather grenades from the bodies of dead Marines.

"Still need some more stuff to throw at those guys," he yelled at Private Don Kelly, one of the few men still alive on the ridge. He threw. He found a loaded BAR in the hands of another fallen Marine, seized it, jumped erect, and fired it until it jammed.

"Nothin' more to give 'em now," the Glory Kid bellowed to Kelly. "Let's get some of these wounded guys down." He bent over to pick up a stricken Marine as easily as hefting his machine gun. "I'll have you in sick bay in no time," he said in a soothing voice, and began walking toward the rear edge of Sugar Loaf. An enemy rifle cracked. Rusty Golar was staggered. He put the wounded man down carefully. Incredulity was etched on his rough, slowly whitening features. He walked to a ditch and sat down in it, pushing back his helmet like a man preparing to take a snooze—and there he died. No posthumous Medal of Honor commemorates the deeds of this valiant warrior, not even another Bronze Star. He had been brave and compassionate, the twin virtues of a born fighter, and though both went unrecognized, Rusty Golar remains a legend in the annals of his gallant corps.

Soon his comrades on Sugar Loaf were recoiling under a thundering shower of enemy mortar shells. Three Sherman tanks that were to have punished the enemy's reverse slope and thus clear the way for the foot soldiers were knocked out by enemy 47 mm antitank guns, their blazing hulks incinerating the silly superstition of the "near-sighted Japanese." Without this support the Marines could not hold against renewed Japanese assaults. They withdrew, leaving behind them the still bodies of about a hundred comrades, among them the burly football star George Murphy, and the forty-five selfless volunteers of the valorous Major Courtney, whose widow would receive his posthumous Medal of Honor.

Throughout that night and the following day the Japanese

clung stubbornly to Sugar Loaf while the entire complex quivered beneath a combined air-sea-land artillery barrage preceding each American assault. But all were repulsed, until, on May 17, an end run turned the Sugar's left flank.

An almost imperceptible depression had been observed running north and south between Half-Moon Hill to the left and Sugar Loaf. It was not actually a valley, but Japanese fire on Marines who had wandered into it had not been heavy or accurate. General Shepherd, up on the lines now, decided to move an entire regiment—the Twenty-ninth—through this tiny chink in Sugar Loaf's armor. Two battalions would go through to strike at Half-Moon Hill, holding there to support another battalion moving against the left face of Sugar Loaf, which their own assault was expected to unmask.

The battalions went forward under a fierce barrage. Half-Moon Hill was hit. Sugar Loaf was attacked. Three times a company of Marines charged to Sugar Loaf's crest. Each time they were driven off. They surged up a fourth time and won. But they had no more ammunition. None could be brought up to them. It was heartbreaking. They had to go down, giving up the vital height taken at a cost of 160 casualties.

The next day they went up to stay.

Four days of full-scale attack, the hammering of two Marine regiments and supporting arms, had worn the complex's defense thin. Sugar Loaf was ready to fall.

Captain Howard Mabie brought his assaulting company up to the edge of the low ground opposite the hill. Artillery and mortars plastered the crest while three tanks slipped around the left flank. The barrage stopped. The Japanese rushed from their caves below the reverse slope to occupy the crest. The tanks took them under fire, surprised them and riddled them.

Rocket trucks raced down from the north, bumping and swaying over a saddle of ground, stopped, loosed their flights of missiles, whirled and careened away with a whine of changing gears and a roar of wasted gasoline—just avoiding the inevitable Japanese artillery shells crashing in behind them. The rockets made Sugar Loaf's hillsides reel and reverberate as though a string of monster firecrackers had been set off. Artillery began again. The Marines sprinted over the field and up Sugar Loaf, one platoon taking the right face, peeling off its fire teams, another sweeping up on the left. They met on the crest, formed, and swept down the reverse slope, killing as they went. Back came the message:

"Send up the PX supplies. Sugar Loaf is ours."

It was—and it wasn't—for it took the fresh Fourth Marines who had relieved the fought-out Twenty-ninth four more days to drive deeper into the complex. The Sixth Marine Division itself lost a total of 2,662 killed and wounded in this bitter battle, with another 1,289 felled by combat fatigue. In the end, after the Half-Moon was taken and the Sixth stood poised to drive down-island into Naha, they came under plunging enemy artillery fire from the left on Shuri Heights.

The Sixth could not strike at Naha until the First destroyed the enemy on Shuri Heights.

The First Marine Division was "processing" its way south.

This was the cold, grim term coined by Major General del Valle to describe the cold, grim warfare that his troops were fighting en route to Shuri Heights. Along that way lay Dakeshi Ridge, Dakeshi Town, Wana Ridge, Wana Draw—those now-familiar formidable jumbles of stone-steel-and-concrete that could only be made smooth by the "processing" of tank-infantry-flamethrower teams. These four places were the sentinel forts guarding the northwest way into the heart of the Naha-Shuri-Yonabaru line at Shuri Castle. Moving down against them, its regiments leapfrogging one another all along the pitiless way, the First Marine Division was exposed to almost constant fire from its left flank and struck unceasingly from its front. The deeper the advance, the more numerous and formidable became the defenses in depth, the more difficult the terrain.

On May 11 the First began bucking at Dakeshi Ridge and Dakeshi Town. Both fell after a seesaw three-day battle, the Americans plodding forward by day, the Japanese counter-attacking by night. Daylight sometimes meant a fresh attack to recover ground surrendered during the night. Platoons took a position at the cost of three-fourths of their men, then tried to hang on with the survivors. Sometimes they could not. In Dakeshi Town the Marines found a labyrinth of tunnels, shafts, and caves, with snipers everywhere among the ruins—crouching behind broken walls, hidden in wells or cisterns. But Dakeshi Town also fell, and on May 14 the First Marine Division entered Wana Draw.

Wana Draw was a long, narrowing ravine running east to Shuri. It was formed by the reverse slope of Wana Ridge on its left and the forward slope of another ridge to the right. All its low, gently rising ground was covered by gunfire, from its mouth four hundred yards wide to the point at which, eight hundred yards east, it narrowed sharply between steep cliffs under the heights of Shuri.

Although neither Shuri nor Shuri Castle was in the zone of the First Marine Division, but rather in the Seventy-seventh Division's, the plunging fire that fell from them was meant for the First Division's left flank. It was necessary for the First to face left, or east, and attack up Wana Draw—both to remove that thorn from its flesh and to knock out those powerful positions menacing the entire western half of the Tenth Army front. Any attack south past Shuri would be struck in both flank and rear.

On May 14, the day on which Major Courtney led the charge on Sugar Loaf, the First Marine Division began "processing" Wana Draw.

A few tanks slipped into the ravine. They probed for the caves. Antitank fire fell on them. Supporting riflemen took the Japanese gunners under fire. Suicide troops rushed for the tanks hurling satchel charges. Again the supporting riflemen protected the tanks. But sometimes the antitank guns knocked out the tanks, sometimes the Japanese infantrymen drove the Marine riflemen back, sometimes the satchel charges blew up a tank. But when the tanks did gain a foothold, then the more vulnerable flame-throwing tanks rumbled in. They sprayed the hillside with fire, particularly those reverse slopes that could not be reached by bombs or artillery.

Squads of foot Marines went in after them, men with bazookas, flamethrowers, hand grenades, blocks of dynamite—peeling off, team by team, taking cave after cave, crawling up to them under the protective fire of riflemen kneeling in the mud. More and more men went into Wana Draw. Day after day the Division bucked against this barrier, but soon there were whole companies working up the slopes, "processing" caves and pillboxes, calling down their mortars and rifle grenades on the machine guns and mortars sure to be nesting on the reverse slope. It was war at its most basic, man to man, a battle fought by corporals and privates. And these were the men who won the Medals of Honor while the First Division processed its way into Shuri: Private Dale Hansen, using a bazooka, a rifle, and hand grenades to knock out a pillbox and a mortar position and kill a dozen Japanese before he lost his own life; Pfc. Albert Schwab, attacking machine guns alone with his flamethrower, silencing them even as he perished; Corporal Louis Hauge, doing the same with grenades, and also dying. With these men were their indomitable comrades of the Navy Medical Corps, men such as Corpsman William Halyburton, who deliberately shielded wounded Marines with his own body until his life leaked out of it.

This was the fight for Wana Draw, that pitiless bloodletting swirling inside a gully while the very elements howled about these men in muddy green floundering up the forward slopes, these men in smeared khaki sliding down the reverse slopes. At night, under cover of smoke screens, the men in khaki crept forward

again to close with the men in green, to fight with bayonets and
fists and strangling hands. But the men in khaki were losing the
fight for Wana Draw. The Marines drew closer to Shuri. The
soldiers of the Seventy-seventh Division on their left were thrust-
ing toward Shuri and Shuri Castle from the eastern gate. On the
east flank the Seventh Infantry Division was back in the line and
smashing into Yonabaru; the Sixth Marine Division was again on
the march to Naha on the west. All along the line, division and
corps artillery were battering Ushijima's strongpoints, the Tenth
Army's Tactical Air Force roved over the battlefield at will—and
the warships of the fleet were slugging away with the most formidable supporting fire yet laid down in the Pacific, for they had
caught the hang of pasting those reverse slopes that land-air
pounding could not reach.

Ushijima's barrier line was buckling.

On the eastern front from Conical Hill to Shuri Castle, the
Ninety-sixth and Seventy-seventh Divisions were also driving
slowly but doggedly into Ushijima's bristling defenses—and with
the Seventy-seventh there marched perhaps the most unusual
hero in the annals of American arms. His name was Pfc. Desmond
Doss. He was a medic in the 307th Infantry. He was also a
Seventh-Day Adventist, a doctrinal pacifist who shrank from even
touching a weapon and would not work on Saturday, his creed's
Sabbath. As a conscientious objector, on religious grounds he
might have joined that corps of noncombatants who refused to
serve their country on the battlefield. But Desmond Doss saw
clearly that it was his duty to serve and that he, too, could risk
his flesh for his country without taking the life of a brother
human.

As a medic during his regiment's bitter battle on the Maeda
Escarpment in late April, Doss distinguished himself by his utter
disregard for his own safety and his devotion to his soldier buddies. Again and again he risked enemy fire to come to the side of

stricken GIs, dressing their wounds and then dragging them to the edge of a cliff, where he fastened them to a rope sling of his own devising and lowered them to safety. He did this so often that some of his buddies, believing that he had a charmed life, sought to stay near him. For his gallantry, Doss received the Medal of Honor: a reproach to those who said, "I will not serve," and a credit to a nation that could bestow its highest military award on a brave pacifist.

Doss was still with the Seventy-seventh on May 11 when that veteran division took on the Chocolate Drop–Wart Hill–Flattop Hill complex in the center of the island. This forbidding position—almost as formidable as Sugar Loaf—bristled with mortars and interlocking machine-guns and 47 mm antitank guns. Because Ushijima had added a protective minefield to its front, the Seventh's GIs—like the Marines at Sugar Loaf—had to attack without tanks. Casualties were frightful. Colonel Aubrey Smith's 306th Regiment was bled so horribly that Smith was compelled to form the remnants—that is, about eight hundred men out of twenty-four hundred—into a single battalion. A similar Gethsemane awaited Colonel Stephen Hamilton's 307th after it relieved the 306th. As Hamilton's soldiers filed into place, one of them thought that the line of American dead sprawled atop Chocolate Drop looked like a skirmish line ready to leap erect and charge.

As Doss had risked his life on the escarpment, he crawled bravely through enemy fire to succor the wounded. But there his charmed life ended when a bursting mortar shell mangled both his legs. Doss treated his own wounds, waiting five hours for stretcher-bearers to arrive. On the way to the Battalion Aid Station, a fierce enemy barrage drove the bearers to cover. Lying alone on the litter, Doss saw a badly wounded GI untended, rolling from the stretcher to crawl to him and dress his wounds. While waiting for the bearers to return, Doss was hit again in the arm, suffering a compound fracture. Overcoming his horror of touching a gun, this indomitable youth actually made a splint for

his arm from a rifle stock, and then squirmed three hundred yards
to the aid station, where he was treated and began to recover from
his wounds.

Such was the uncommon valor mixed with unique compassion
that was common on Okinawa.

On the Twenty-fourth Corps's eastern flank above Buckner
Bay the Ninety-sixth Division was driving against Conical Hill,
and also Dick Hill just to the east of Flattop. Here stiff resistance
had stalled both GIs of the Seventy-seventh on their division's
extreme left and those of the Ninety-sixth on their own right. But
on May 17 an infantry platoon entered over a road cut between
Dick and Flattop to explode enemy mines. They used bayonets
to detonate the buried explosives—a risky tactic that cost nineteen
casualties. In the process they sealed off five caves full of enemy
soldiers.

Lieutenant Colonel Cyril Sterner of the 382nd's Second Battalion realized at once that this lightly defended road was the key
to the Japanese position. But it was heavily mined. Ingeniously,
Sterner ordered seven tons of bangalore torpedoes—lengths of
pipe packed with explosives—laid in the road's ruts and detonated, thus blasting all the mines. Now tanks could get into the
rear of Dick and Flattop, assisted by flamethrowing tanks, and
once the Americans were able to make such a penetration they
always turned the enemy flank. That was what was done at Flattop
and Dick, and by May 21 all that was needed for the Tenth Army
to pierce Ushijima's barrier line was for Colonel Eddy May's
382nd Infantry of the Ninety-sixth Division to crack that hard
nut known as Conical Hill.

Conical Hill was the eminence holding down the easternmost
flank of Ushijima's Naha-Shuri-Yonabaru barrier. If it fell to the
Americans, it would unmask Yonabaru, the eastern terminus of
the vital Yonabaru-Naha highway. If the Twenty-fourth Corps

did succeed in turning it, its troops could then meet the two Marine divisions of the Third Corps at Naha, thus effecting a double envelopment that might trap Ushijima before he could retreat farther south. Because of the importance of this position, General Hodge had chosen Colonel May—his best regimental commander—to direct the attack.

Conical Hill's importance had not been lost on General Ushijima, and he had stationed one thousand of his finest troops there, confident that they could not be dislodged. Most of them were concentrated in the hills and ridges to the west of Conical, where they expected the enemy to strike. Indeed, that was where May actually attempted his penetration. But the battalion May had assigned to that sector got nowhere in ten days of fighting, while another assaulting Conical's north face had seized so much ground in two days that both Hodge and Buckner were delighted.

Buckner actually joined May on May 13 to watch the Shermans blasting away at every fissure and crack of Conical's forward slope. Now E and F Companies of Lieutenant Colonel Edward Stare's Second Battalion began to move out. Because E was slow getting started, the two platoons forming the spearhead of Lieutenant Owen O'Neill's F Company quickly reached their jump-off point. As an indication of the heavy casualties ravaging the Ninety-sixth's company officers, these units were commanded by two technical sergeants: Guy Dale and Dennis Doniphan. They waited for O'Neill, unaware that his radio was not working. Unwilling to delay longer, they went up Conical on their own initiative. There was little resistance, but the Americans were not deceived. Forward slopes were always a waltz: the real dance of death came screeching out the back door. Yet, to their surprise, not a soldier was hit as they climbed to a point about fifty feet below Conical's high round peak. Here they began to dig in, for to attempt to take Conical's tiny indefensible top would have drawn fire from every quarter.

By one of those accidental strokes of luck that so often rule the battlefield, Doniphan and Dale apparently had caught the Japanese in an unguarded moment. Perhaps the enemy had been preoccupied with those western hills. Whatever the excuse, the Americans had been given time to entrench themselves—and it was the *chink* and *clink* of those entrenching tools that alarmed Lieutenant Colonel Kensuke Udo. At once he ordered a counterattack. Out of the reverse slope poured the yelling Japanese, coming full tilt down the forward slope to be hammered to the ground. Now Lieutenant O'Neill joined his men, visibly and vocally pleased by the action of his alert sergeants, immediately calling for the tardy E Company under Captain Stanley Sutten to come up the hill and form a battle front on F Company's right flank. Two full companies safely entrenched and supported by mortars below now held a perimeter east of Conical's peak. Oddly enough, the Japanese did not counter-attack that night.

At 383rd's headquarters a delighted Simon Bolivar Buckner congratulated Colonel May on what he described as one of the finest small-unit maneuvers he had ever witnessed.

During the next three days—May 14, 15, and 16—E and F Companies, now joined by G, fought off the desperately counterattacking Japanese in a bitter battle on Conical's forward slope. Gradually the enemy—again charging through their own mortar shells—began to whittle Colonel Stare's battalion. At last Major General Jim Bradley ordered Lieutenant Colonel Daniel Nolan's Third Battalion of the 381st Infantry to relieve Stare's valiant but fought-out Dogfaces. It was a wise decision, for the belligerent Nolan sent his GIs driving down a hogback into Sugar Hill, and with the fall of that strongpoint, Conical Hill was in American hands.

In ten days between May 11 and 21 both sides had been locked in the fiercest fighting of this terrible Okinawa campaign, so hideously reminiscent of the trench warfare of World War I, both in its horrible human losses and the attempt of one side to pierce the defenses of an enemy determined to yield not an inch.

It was the unstoppable force against the immovable object; more clearly in military terms, what always happens when firepower wielded by the valiant cannot fail to overwhelm spiritual power alone—no matter how valorous and dedicated its devotees. Casualties in the Seventy-seventh Division were 239 killed, 1,212 wounded, and 16 missing; in the Ninety-sixth Division 138 killed, 1,059 wounded, and 9 missing. Japanese losses are not known, although they were probably twice this number, even though Ushijima's soldiers were on the defensive.

Perhaps the greatest tribute to the American fighting men on Okinawa came from their favorite English-language broadcaster, Radio Tokyo:

> Sugar Loaf Hill . . . Chocolate Drop . . . Strawberry Hill. Gee, these places sound wonderful! You can just see the candy houses with the white picket fences around them and the candy canes hanging from the trees, their red and white stripes glistening in the sun. But the only thing red about these places is the blood of Americans. Yes, sir, these are the names of hills in southern Okinawa where the fighting's so close that you can get down to bayonets and sometimes your bare fists . . . I guess it's natural to idealize the worst places with pretty names to make them seem less awful. Why, Sugar Loaf has changed hands so often it looks like Dante's Inferno. Yes, sir, Sugar Loaf Hill . . . Chocolate Drop . . . Strawberry Hill. They sound good, don't they? Only those who've been there know what they're really like.

True enough. But only the Yanks who were there really knew the final score.

Ushijima Retreats Again

CHAPTER TWENTY-ONE

Major General John Hodge saw the lodgment on Conical Hill as an opportunity for a turning movement of Ushijima's eastern flank. He would use the rested Seventy-seventh Division—"rested" in that, withdrawn from combat, they had only to contend with mud, misery, and malaria—to move along Buckner Bay's coastal flats without fear of plunging fire from Conical Hill. If the Seventy-seventh could reach and capture Yonabaru, they could wheel west to join the Marine divisions moving around the enemy's western flank and so trap the Thirty-second Army in a double envelopment.

It was an excellent concept and a distinct possibility, although two factors stood between the idea and its execution: renewed rain and Ushijima's unwillingness to sit still for destruction.

On the night of May 22, with the Sixth Marine Division across the Asato River and poised to break into Naha, there was another conference under Shuri Castle. Lieutenant General Ushijima had decided to retreat. He could no longer hold his Yonabaru-Shuri-Naha line. He would have to withdraw south of the Yonabaru-Naha valley, abandoning even that fine cross-island road. Where to? Should it be the wild, roadless Chinen Peninsula on the east coast, or southernmost Kiyamu Peninsula? The wrangle began. In the end, the Kiyamu was chosen because of the strength of the Yaeju-Yuza Peaks and the honeycombs of natural and artificial caves that could accommodate the entire Thirty-second Army for its final stand.

The next day Ushijima began reinforcing his flanks again to hold off the Americans while his withdrawal began, but he was too late to prevent the turning of the west flank at Naha. The Sixth Division burst into the city's ruins and began its reduction.

Ushijima still counter-attacked the Seventh Division on the east flank at Yonabaru, trying to relieve the pressure there, but the Seventh's valiant Dogfaces held fast.

A nocturnal *kamikaze* raid hurled at Okinawa shipping to co-incide with Ushijima's land strikes was shattered, with 150 planes shot down in exchange for the loss of the destroyer-transport *Bates* and one LSM, plus damage to eight other ships.

The most ferocious display of antiaircraft power yet seen in the Pacific broke up a daring airborne attack on Yontan and Kadena Airfields. It was an unusually clear night, and there were thousands of witnesses to this small savage setback that the suicide spirit was able to inflict on the Americans.

Perhaps twenty twin-engined bombers came gliding through a fiery lacework woven by American antiaircraft gunners. Eleven of them fell in flames. The rest, except one, fled.

That solitary Sally bomber skidded on its belly along one of Yontan's runways. When it stopped, eight of fourteen men of the Japanese First Air Raiding Brigade were dead in their seats, but six of them were alive, tumbling out the door, coming erect, and sprinting for parked planes while hurling heat grenades and phosphorous bombs. They blew up eight airplanes, damaged twenty-six others, destroyed two fuel dumps housing seventy thousand gallons of gasoline, and killed two Marines and wounded eighteen others before they were finally hunted down and killed.

In the morning the Tenth Army was still grinding down toward the heart of Ushijima's defense in Shuri Castle. Marines of the First Division in Wana Draw began to draw swiftly closer to the city and its heights to their east. They began to notice Japanese sealing off caves and quitting the draw. At noon of May 26 Major General del Valle asked for an aerial reconnaissance over the Yonabaru-Naha valley. He had a hunch the Japanese were pulling back from Shuri, trying to sneak out under cover of a heavy rain.

A spotter plane from the battleship *New York* reported that the roads behind Shuri were packed. Between three thousand and four thousand Japanese were on the rear march with all their guns, tanks, and trucks. In thirteen minutes, despite rain and bad visibility, the warships of the fleet were on the target. Soon fifty Marine Corsairs were with them, rocketing and strafing, and every Marine artillery piece or mortar within range had its smoking muzzle pointed toward the valley. They killed from five hundred to eight hundred Japanese and littered the muddy roadways with wrecked vehicles.

Three days later the Marines took Shuri Castle.

It was not supposed to be theirs to take; it was the objective of the Seventy-seventh Division, the very plum of the Okinawa fighting, but the First Marine Division took it anyway.

General del Valle sent a battalion of the Fifth Marines climbing into Shuri on May 29. He wanted to get around and behind the Japanese still holding out in Wana Draw. The First Battalion quickly stormed Shuri Ridge to the east, or left, of the draw—so quickly that Lieutenant Colonel Charles Shelburne asked permission to go on to the castle eight hundred yards east. Del Valle granted it. The Seventy-seventh Division was still two days' hard fighting from the castle, and the chance was too good to ignore. The light defenses around Shuri might be only a temporary lapse.

Company A of the Fifth Marines under Captain Julius Dusenbury began slogging east in knee-deep mud. Inside Captain

Dusenbury's helmet was a flag, as had become almost customary among Marine commanders since the Suribachi flag-raising. While the Marines marched, del Valle was just barely averting the Seventy-seventh's planned artillery and aerial strike on Shuri Castle, and then Dusenbury's Marines overran a party of Japanese soldiers and swept into the castle courtyard, into the battered ruins of what had once been a beautiful palace with curving, tiered roofs of tile. They ran up to its high parapet, and over this Captain Dusenbury flew his flag.

Shuri Castle, the key bastion of the Okinawa defenses, was in American hands—and if the Seventy-seventh Division was irritated, if the Tenth Army was displeased, the soldier who commanded the Americans on Okinawa could not be entirely annoyed. The flag that Captain Dusenbury of South Carolina flew was the flag of Simon Bolivar Buckner's father. The Stars and Bars, not the Stars and Stripes, waved over Okinawa.

Two days later Old Glory was in its rightful place. General del Valle sent a party with the standard of the First Marine Division, the one that had flown over Guadalcanal, New Britain, and Peleliu.

Now, above Shuri Castle not far from the spot where Commodore Perry had hoisted the American flag a century ago, the most victorious flag of the Pacific was caught and flung in the breeze.

The Japanese retreating to the south could see it. They fired on it, missing. They kept firing, for they understood that the terrible power it symbolized was already massing to come south and destroy them.

Chrysanthemums Die
in Sea and Sky

CHAPTER TWENTY-TWO

Plane and pilot losses in the Fifth Air Fleet and Sixth Air Army had been so severe that in Japan a special *kamikaze* corps had been organized. Replacements in both machines and men were fed from bases in central and northern Nippon to Kyushu. Often these aviators were hardly more than raw recruits whose training periods were of short duration. At first the *kamikaze* had been strictly volunteers, but as the Okinawa campaign continued, all Japanese sailors and soldiers were subject to suicide duty whether or not they wished to go. Sometimes commanders "volunteered" their entire units for this not-always desirable service. More and more "glorious young eagles" began to "get lost" and returned to base. Others who went willingly were frustrated by frequent engine trouble or the weather. These were the ardent, idealist youths such as the pilot who left the verse: "When I fly the skies / What a fine burial place / Would be the top of a cloud." Others were not so eager to make the supreme sacrifice, like the one who wrote: "I say frankly, I do not die willingly. I die not without regret. My country's future leaves me uneasy . . . I am terribly distressed."

Much of the glamour of the Special Attack Forces had faded. Its members were still idolized, of course, and there was always a ceremony for the final departure: toasts of *sake* to be drunk and cigarettes from the Imperial Gift to be smoked—Hirohito's parting benefaction upon his private army of assassins. But the scourging of the Kyushu bases by American air power had turned these once-thriving and stimulating centers into dreary, dismal limbos where the *kamikaze* awaiting the death order escaped boredom—or depression—by helping local farmers with their spring planting.

Rain, it seemed, always brought the *kamikaze*, and on May 11 as the Tenth Army assault slogged and slipped forward, the growl and grumble and whistling rain of the Great Loo Choo's skies were a welcome sound to about 150 Japanese aircraft hurtling south from Kyushu. Those who were believing Shintoists said a prayer of thanksgiving to the Sun Goddess for having providentially averted her face, forgetting in their gratitude the disaster that had crippled their attack at its outset. A formation of Judy bombers climbing from Kokobu Airfield's Airstrip 2 crashed into a formation of Val suiciders taking off from another runway, with a total loss of 15 planes. The remaining 135, however, continued to roar south for Okinawa and TF 58.

Those that reached Picket Station 15 about 7:50 A.M. were delighted to sight two enemy destroyers clearly visible below them. They were the *Evans* and *Hugh W. Hadley*, commanded by Naval Academy classmates Commanders Robert Archer in *Evans* and Baron Mullaney in *Hadley*. They watched in apprehension as no less than 50 suiciders peeled off to begin orbiting above them—and when they began to dive, there ensued probably the classic ship-airplane battle of World War II.

For an hour and a half without letup *Evans* and *Hadley* fought off fifty *kamikaze*. *Hadley* alone shot down twenty-three of them, while *Evans* claimed fifteen. The Marines from Yontan and Kadena knocked another nineteen out of the skies. Commander

Mullaney of *Hadley* called for Marines to help him. Back came the squadron leader's answer: "I'm out of ammunition but I'm sticking with you." He did, flying straight into a flurry of ten *kamikaze* coming at *Hadley* fore and aft, trying to head them off—while other Marines of his squadron rode down through the ack-ack with stuttering guns. They were not always successful, for both of these tough little ships took four *kamikaze* hits apiece. But they survived to be towed to that anchorage in Kerama-retto that had become a vast hospital ward for stricken and maimed American ships, and there Commander Mullaney could write this tribute to the Yontan and Kadena fliers: "I am willing to take my ship to the shores of Japan if I could have these Marines with me."

Meanwhile, another fifty *kamikaze* had found Task Force Fifty-eight. On the bridge of his flag carrier *Bunker Hill* Admiral Marc Mitscher watched in open admiration as the Japanese pilots skillfully used rain clouds and window to deceive the American radar. He frowned as a Zero suicider broke from low clouds on the carrier's starboard quarter, smashing through rows of planes on the flight deck to start fires before crashing overboard and exploding. Behind it came a Judy diving straight down from astern. It hit at the worst possible moment—with armed planes refueling on the flight deck. While a broken fuel line fed a roaring fire, these planes exploded like a burst from a giant machine gun. In a few moments 400 sailors were killed or blown out of sight and another 264 wounded.

Even so *Bunker Hill*'s ordeal did not quite equal the agony of *Franklin*, although there was just as much heroism in the fight to douse her flames and keep her afloat. Machinist's Mate Jack Salvaggio would forever bless the porthole in the ship's stencil room that he had so fervently cursed for the wind blowing through it to scatter his papers. Now he wriggled through this passport to continued life. Another machinist named Harold Fraught believed he was trapped in a smoke-filled passageway, until he saw a tiny open porthole. "I was about to reach it but couldn't, and I was just about to give up when someone pushed me through. I sure would like to find out who it was who kept pushing every guy through but not saving himself."

For 5½ hours *Bunker Hill*'s gallant crew fought the flames threatening to consume and sink their ship. Splendid seamanship saved her: heeling from a list to starboard to one to port, the great vessel gradually combined gravity and gathering momentum to send a huge mass of burning gasoline and oil, water and foam, sloshing slowly from the hangar deck overboard into the sea. At this point, Admiral Mitscher transferred his flag from *Bunker Hill*—the second-worst-hit ship in the Navy to survive, though she would need many months of repair—to the more famous *Enterprise*. Next day, the *kikusui* struck again, but not nearly with as much savagery as on May 11—scoring only one hit on the *Bache*, a radar picket ship far south of Okinawa, knocking out its power plant and killing forty-one sailors.

Nevertheless Admiral Spruance was alarmed by the renewed fury of the Floating Chrysanthemums and ordered Mitscher to take two task groups north to work over the Kyushu airfields. Mitscher did, introducing a naval novelty in the night-flying Air Group Ninety aboard *Enterprise*, which gave the weary Japanese airmen no rest. Mitscher also struck hard at Ugaki's northern airfields, shifting his sights from the enemy's battered southern bases. Meanwhile, Corsairs and Hellcats ranged among enemy interceptors like devouring wolves while the torpedo-launching Avengers and Helldiver dive-bombers ravaged no less than thirty-four of Ugaki's air bases.

Still the *kamikaze* fought back. On May 14 a flight of eighty-four fighters zoomed aloft as cover for twenty-six Zero suiciders bent on punishing TF 58 for its audacious strikes at the home-land. A pretakeoff briefing could not have been briefer: three words, "Get the carriers!" Young Lieutenant Tomai Kai could not forget this command as he roared aloft in his bomb-laden

Zero. To his delight he soon found himself above TF 58 and a monster carrier. He had no way of knowing that this was *Enterprise*—the *"Big E,"* one of the most battle-seasoned flattops of World War II—but he didn't hesitate to jump her despite the bucking and bouncing of his frail craft from enemy ack-ack exploding around him. Bursting from a cloud at fifteen hundred feet, Kai pointed his Zero's nose at the *Big E*'s stern and opened his throttle, miraculously passing unscathed through a storm of 20 and 40 mm tracers flowing toward him. Standing on the carrier's bridge Admiral Mitscher's calculating eye calmly watched the enemy's approach.

Two hundred yards astern Lieutenant Kai flip-flopped his aircraft upside down just as he passed over *Enterprise*, and then, to steepen his dive, yanked the stick all the way back. Just before he crashed into the carrier's flight deck at an angle of fifty degrees, he released his 550-pound bomb. The missile plunged straight down the yawning elevator well, exploding with a monstrous roar that sent the elevator roof spinning lazily into the sea. Fortunately, most of the crewmen above deck were wearing flash-proof clothing so that only a few men were badly burned in comparison to the horrible scorching of *Franklin*'s crewmen. Moreover, only thirteen were killed and sixty-nine wounded. *Big E*'s alert crewmen had prepared their ship for attack. Fuel lines had been drained and filled with CO_2; aircraft had been disarmed, drained of fuel, and stowed below; compartments had been made watertight by dogging down the bulkheads, and emergency rations were stored within them. Best of all, when flames did erupt, the fire-fighting details were ready for them.

Thus, when Admiral Mitscher on his flag bridge stared quizzically at the hole left in the flight deck by Kai's Zero, he was not dismayed. Instead, he removed the long-visored baseball cap he always wore, scratched his bald head and said: "Tell my task group commanders that if the Japanese keep this up, they're going to grow hair on my head yet." Marc Mitscher also would cherish

a calling card found on the intact corpse of the heroic young
Lieutenant Tomai Kai who had come so close to sinking the admiral's flagship.

Following the failure of the Floating Chrysanthemum operation that included the airborne attack on Yontan-Kadena and
Lieutenant Kai's crash dive on *Enterprise*, the Fifth Air Fleet was
so short of planes and pilots that it pressed into service twenty
Shirigaku twin-engine trainers. These awkward aircraft, certainly
no match for the swift and sturdy American fighters, comprised
most of the aircraft deployed in *Kikusui* 7 on May 24. No decision
could have been more indicative of the desperation of Ugaki and
Sugahara. They would not only lose the invaluable pilots and
crew-trainers of the Shirigaku, but have few instructors remaining
to teach the low-quality recruits being dragooned in the north
and sent to Kyushu. And they did lose them, as the Marine Corsairs roved among them with stuttering guns. Nevertheless,
Kikusui 7 did hole the destroyer *Stormes*, while damaging the
destroyer-transports *Bates* and *Barry* so badly that *Bates* sank and
Barry was converted to a *kamikaze* decoy.

But the Divine Winds were back on May 27–28 for Floating
Chrysanthemum 8, a novelty in that on the twenty-seventh some
eighty-five Army and Navy aircraft attacked at night. Here was a
demonstration of how inept aircraft designed for daytime combat
can be fighting in darkness. Picket destroyers *Anthony* and *Braine*
firing on radar quickly took out an indefinite number of invisible
assailants, identified only by gasoline fires on black water. Wisely,
the others waited until dawn to renew the assault, slightly damaging *Anthony* and mangling *Braine* to kill about a hundred American seamen and wounding about the same number.

The next day in clearing weather the *kikusui* were back, this
time swooping again on their favorite target: the ships of Radar
Picket Station 15. Destroyers *Drexler* and *Lowry* were hit and
staggered, but above them Marine Corsairs were plucking petals

from the Chrysanthemums. Lieutenants R. F. Bourne and J. B.
Seaman each downed a red-balled enemy, while Seaman exploded
a third. As both pilots joined to attack a fourth, peeling the enemy's metal hide, its pilot maintained control and plunged into
Drexler with an impact that sent flames shooting hundreds of feet
high. Within a minute *Drexler* rolled over and sank, taking 158
men down with her.

Reports of this disaster made eyelids flutter in Washington.
Had the enemy perfected a new and fearful explosive? The answer
came from a board of inquiry that preferred to believe—and
probably correctly—that a heavy bomb striking a ship's magazine
could easily produce such a violent fireball.

After May 28, Admiral Ugaki fully intended to continue his
kikusui attacks, still believing that Admiral Spruance now commanded a ghost fleet of floating wrecks and derelicts. But then
bad weather and the Army's disenchantment with the Floating
Chrysanthemums—the generals had always believed that Japanese air power should be husbanded for homeland defense—in-
terfered with his plans. To his dismay General Sugahara and his
Sixth Air Army were removed from Navy control. He still had
the cooperation of the Army's Third Air Division, however, and
planned to resume what can only be described as his Graveyard
Operation with *Kikusui* 9 on June 3.

Before then American airpower received a powerful rein-
forcement—in the arrival of a squadron of Army P-47 Thunderbolts. Here was a fighter unrivaled for its speed, armament,
armor, and climbing power. On May 28 a flight of eight Thunderbolts under Captain John Vogt jumped twenty-eight Zeros
forming in a Lufbery circle—a defensive aerial tactic perhaps
copied from a ring of show horses moving tail to nose. Thus,
each Zero was to protect the tail of the plane ahead. Because the
Zero with its light armament and thin armor was fast and ma-
neuverable, these pilots probably thought they were safe from
attack, but the Thunderbolts climbing at full throttle moved high

above their quarry at twenty-eight thousand feet—and then came screaming down in a dive that sent six of the enemy flaming into the sea along with two "probables." Captain Vogt claimed to have accounted for five of them.

Floating Chrysanthemum 9 did take to the skies on June 3, supposedly with about 101 aircraft. But this seems unlikely. The naval historian Samuel Eliot Morison gives only fifty. Whatever their number it was sharply reduced by the Yontan-Kadena Marine Corsairs, succeeding only in holing a minelayer. The next day the *kamikaze* dove again, but in almost negligible strength. Once again the unfortunate *Anthony* was their target. To the crew's unbelieving eyes a suicider barely nicked by gunfire actually *bailed out*! This most unwarlike tactic, however, availed him nothing: his parachute streamed after him unopened to mark his plunge into the briny. Another plane dived at *Anthony* but her 40 mm gunners shot it down.

Kikusui 9 suggested that attrition of the Fifth Air Fleet—raids from Okinawa, Iwo Jima, Guam, and the fast carriers—was almost complete. Admiral Ugaki, who had started in April with a fleet of more than 4,000 aircraft, was now in June down to about 1,270, of which only 570 were serviceable—and these marked for conventional duty. Only a handful of *kamikaze* remained. Nevertheless this relentless—not to say merciless—air admiral prepared Floating Chrysanthemum 10. With Okinawa already doomed, it was scheduled for June 21–22.

Supposedly fifty-eight to forty-five *kamikaze* had been collected, escorted by an unknown number of fighters. Also aboard were six *baka* bombs, Ugaki's masterpiece. How many of them "aborted" and returned to base is not known; but by late June "abortion" was becoming nearly as popular as divine death had been. This last attack of the deadly Floating Chrysanthemums produced only a few near misses while one faithful suicider set the seaplane tender *Curtis* afire and another struck at *Barry*—the previously damaged destroyer-escort converted to decoy duty—

as it was being towed to its station by LSM-50—sinking both ships. Meanwhile the *baka* brigade was a complete fizzle: two failed to release from their mother planes and were returned to Kyushu while the other four were either lost when their mother planes were shot down or harmed nothing but a few dozen fishes. Thus the inglorious end of the *kikusui* that were to save Japan.

Japan's third Divine Wind had spent itself on the sturdy ships and stout hearts of the United States Naval Service.

Ushijima's Last Stand

CHAPTER TWENTY-THREE

It was the month of June, the month of Ushijima's last stand.

Lieutenant General Buckner had redisposed his Tenth Army for the final heave of the war. On the west, or right, flank the Marines' sector had been narrowed. The Sixth Marine Division was going to make a shore-to-shore amphibious assault on the Oroku Peninsula in the southwest, and the First Marine Division had not the strength to cover the entire Third Corps front.

The Third Corps, in fact, was depleted. With the Second Marine Division sent back to Saipan—rather than kept afloat as a *kamikaze* target—Major General Geiger had not been able to rest either the First or the Sixth. He had no reserve, and the divisions themselves had tried to maintain battle efficiency by resting one regiment while the other two attacked. But it could not always be done. So the Third Corps needed troops, and soon the Eighth Regiment of the Second Marine Division would be brought into Okinawa to furnish them. But this was not until after the Eighth had finished capturing islands to the west of Okinawa to give Admiral Turner long-range radar and fighter-director stations.

The Twenty-fourth Corps was in better shape. Major General Hodge had three divisions—exclusive of the Twenty-seventh on garrison in the north—and had been able to rest one while the other two were attacking. Only infrequently, as in the final days before Shuri, were all three in the line. But from June 4 onward the Twenty-fourth Corps was grinding down on the Yaeju-Yuza Peaks where most of the Thirty-second Army's remnants had holed up. Even General Ushijima was here, conducting the last stand from his headquarters cave just above the ocean.

June 5 was a sad day for General Hodge, for on that date his favorite regimental commander—Colonel Eddy May—fell dead with an enemy machine gunner's bullet through his heart. Hodge had called May "the finest soldier I have ever known," and though he was indeed "a hard 'un," the courageous calm with which he would stand exposed to enemy fire while studying Japanese positions was legendary. Two weeks later the Ninety-sixth Division lost another brave leader: Brigadier General Claudius Easley, assistant division commander. As usual this brave little gamecock was up front scouting the enemy, and just as he pointed out an enemy machine gun, a burst from that very weapon pierced his brain.

On the same day that Easley was killed the final Medal of Honor was won on Okinawa. Technical Sergeant John Meagher of the Seventy-seventh's 305th Infantry was mounted on a tank directing its fire when a Japanese soldier wielding a satchel charge rushed at him. Dropping to the ground, Meagher bayoneted his assailant, then ran back to his Sherman to fire a machine gun at a pair of Japanese machine guns. Emptying his gun's belt, Meagher seized his thirty-five-pound weapon as though it were a baseball bat to club the remaining enemy gunners to death.

Casualties in the Ninety-sixth had been far from light as the division ground south on the honeycomb of caves and fortified peaks that was the Yaeju-Yuza. Its rifle battalions were so reduced in strength that General Hodge, to maintain the division's momentum, transferred the Seventy-seventh's 305th Infantry to the Ninety-sixth.

When the GIs of the Twenty-fourth Corps began to penetrate the enemy cave strongholds, many of them were sickened with what they found. The caves were full of men and misery. There were many sick and dying. Some caves had become reeking pest-holes. As many as forty men lay in some of these hillside warrens. At times a doctor or a corpsman came around to ask how they felt. They could do little more. They had no supplies. Men died from wounds not considered serious. Filth accumulated. The rain drummed outside, water streamed into the caves, and the wounded nearly drowned. The smell was so overpowering that men could hardly breathe.

Still Ushijima was determined to fight on. He shared the fanaticism of those Army diehards who were even then, in that month of June, attempting to wreck the peace party that the new premier, Baron Kantaro Suzuki, was forming with the secret encouragement of Emperor Hirohito. Tokyo had been savaged twice more, on May 23 and 25, and the emperor was now genuinely dismayed by the slaughter among his people.

But General Ushijima and General Cho, resuming their old relationship, were capable of no such dismay. The fight was to be to the finish, and on June 4 the Tenth Army shuddered and drove forward.

On that date the Sixth Marine Division's spearheads shoved off from Naha to make the last Marine amphibious assault of World War II. Again the amtracks, wallowing in the sea waves, the naval gunfire thundering overhead, the shores of the objective winking and spouting smoke—and in they went to conquer three-by-two Oroku Peninsula in a whirling ten-day battle. Again beaches, coral pinnacles, caves, hills, tunnel systems, 5,000 last-ditch Japanese to be killed, an admiral to be driven to suicide, and again death and wounds for Marines—1,608 of them. Oroku was the Pacific War in microcosm—even in its Medals of Honor:

Private Robert McTureous attacking machine guns firing on stretcher-bearers and losing his life to save his buddies; Corpsman Fred Lester continuing to treat wounded Marines while dying of his own wounds. But Oroku ended in a rout after Admiral Ota committed *hara-kiri*. On June 13 the Japanese threw down their arms and fled toward the mainland in the southeast. They could not escape. The First Marine Division had driven past the base of the peninsula and sealed it off. The Japanese began surrendering.

Beneath Oroku, the First had broken through to the south coast. Okinawa had been sliced down the middle, but more important to those weary, hungry Marines who did it was the sea outlet to which amtracks could now bring supplies. The men had been a week on reduced rations, slogging through the mud that made supply nearly impossible.

On the eastern flank the Seventh and Ninety-sixth Infantry Divisions were also nearing the southern coast. Lieutenant General Buckner had already made a surrender appeal to Ushijima. He had had a letter dropped behind the lines. It said:

> The forces under your command have fought bravely and well, and your infantry tactics have merited the respect of your opponents . . . Like myself, you are an infantry general long schooled and practiced in infantry warfare . . . I believe, therefore, that you understand as clearly as I, that the destruction of all Japanese resistance on the island is merely a matter of days . . .

The letter was dropped on June 10. It reached Ushijima and Cho on June 17. They thought it hilarious. How could a *Samurai* surrender? A *Samurai* can only kill himself.

Ushijima and Cho had already resigned themselves to *hara-kiri* by that seventeenth of June, for by then all was over. On the west flank the First Marine Division was battling through Kunishi

Ridge while the Sixth had again come into line on the right and was racing for Ara Point, the southernmost tip of Okinawa. In the east, the Ninety-sixth Division was finishing off resistance in the Yaeju-Yuza Peaks, and the Seventh Division's soldiers were closing in on the Thirty-second Army's very headquarters.

There was nothing left for Ushijima and Cho, save the satisfying news the next day that the American who had insulted them with a surrender offer was himself dead.

Simon Bolivar Buckner had come down to Mezado Ridge to see the fresh Eighth Marine Regiment enter battle. The Eighth had come to Okinawa on June 15, after seizing Admiral Turner's radar outposts, and was attached to the First Division. As had happened in the beginning at Guadalcanal, when another regiment of the Second Division was attached to the First, so it was happening in the end at Okinawa.

Colonel Clarence Wallace sent the Eighth Marines in at Kunishi Ridge. They were to attack in columns of battalions to seize a road, to split the enemy in two, to carry out General del Valle's plans for a decisive thrust to the sea. Lieutenant General Buckner joined Colonel Wallace on Mezado Ridge at noon. He watched the Marines for about an hour. They moved swiftly on their objective. Buckner said:

"Things are going so well here, I think I'll move on to another unit."

Five Japanese shells struck Mezado Ridge. They exploded and filled the air with flying coral. A shard pierced General Buckner's chest and he died within ten minutes—knowing, at least, that his Tenth Army was winning.

Command went to Roy Geiger, senior officer and about to be promoted to lieutenant general. The grizzled white bear who had been at Guadalcanal in the beginning was leading at the end on Okinawa.

That came three days later.

On June 21 a patrol from the Sixth Marine Division reached a small mound atop a spiky coral cliff. It was the tip of Ara Point. Beneath them were the mingling waters of the Pacific Ocean and the East China Sea.

A few more days of skirmishing and a reverse mop-up drive to the north remained. When these were over, and the last of the *kamikaze* had been shot down, the Japanese Thirty-second Army was no more, with roughly 100,000 dead, and, surprisingly, another 10,000 captured. American casualties totaled 49,151, with Marine losses at 2,938 dead or missing and 13,708 wounded; the Army's at 4,675 and 18,099; and the Navy's at 4,907 and 4,824. There was little left of Japanese airpower after losses of about 3,000 planes*—about 1,900 of them *kamikaze*—against 763 for the Americans; and the sinking of *Yamato* and 15 other ships meant the end of Nippon's Navy. Though the United States Navy had been staggered with 36 ships sunk and another 368 damaged, there were still plenty left to mount the fall invasion of Kyushu from Okinawa.

So the Great Loo Choo fell to the Americans after eighty-three days of fighting. A few hours after the Marine patrol reached Ara Point, Major General Geiger declared organized resistance to be at an end.

---

* Official and early American estimates of 7,800 Japanese planes lost during the Okinawa Campaign—either in combat or under enemy air raids—were much too high. A more conservative and probably more accurate figure of 3,000 was later made by the U.S. Strategic Bombing Survey.

A *Samurai* Farewell

On the night of June 21—the day General Geiger declared the American victory on Okinawa—Ushijima and Cho realized in their headquarters under Hill 95 near the Pacific Ocean that the end had come. Soldiers of Colonel John Finn's Thirty-second Infantry of the Seventh Division were still dropping hand grenades through a vertical air shaft from the top of the hill. The explosives had already killed or wounded ten officers. Neither Ushijima nor Cho wished to meet a similar fate at the hands of the American devils. They would take their own lives in the accepted *Samurai* ceremony.

Colonel Yahara had desired to join them in *hara-kiri*, but Ushijima had decreed that his planning officer, with his excellent memory and habit of straightforward reporting, should be the only man to attempt to escape to Tokyo with a full account of what had happened on Okinawa. Unfortunately, in his physique and bearing, Hiromichi Yahara was also the worst possible choice. No matter how he sought to disguise himself, this tall and patrician officer would stand out among the diminutive Okinawan population like a green tree in a petrified forest—and he was quickly captured. Being a *Samurai*, he had probably asked for a bayonet with which to make the act of expiation like so many other captured *Samurai* before him. If he had, he certainly would have been laughingly refused.

That night under Hill 95 Lieutenant Generals Ushijima and Cho, together with their ranking officers, consumed a farewell dinner prepared for them by the commander's cook, Tetsuo Nakamuta. It began with bean-curd soup, and then proceeded to a bountiful repast of rice, canned meats, potatoes, fried fish cakes, fresh cabbage, and a dessert of canned pineapple. *Sake* flowed as freely as the lively conversation. At the meal's end Isamo Cho produced from his large stock of liquors a bottle of Black and White scotch, with which he and his chief solemnly toasted each other. It was agreed that nothing should be allowed to interfere with the ritual suicide of Ushijima and Cho.

Thus, in the early morning hours just before moonrise, the officers and men of Thirty-second Army Headquarters would deliver the last Banzai of World War II: a climbing charge up Hill 95, and after that, if there were any survivors, the town of Mabuni.

At about 3 A.M. of June 22, 1945, with a glowing white moon polishing the gleaming black waters of the Pacific—and with Ushijima's staff singing *"Umi Yukaba"*—the members of the last Banzai began climbing the cliff.

Behind them at his desk Ushijima wrote his last message to Tokyo: "Our strategy, tactics and techniques all were used to the utmost. We fought valiantly, but it was as nothing before the material strength of the enemy." Cho wrote: "22nd day, 6th month, 20th year of the Showa Era. I depart without regret, fear, shame or obligations. Army Chief of Staff Cho; Army Lieutenant General Cho, Isamu, age of departure 52 years. At this time and place I hereby certify the foregoing."

Bowing to his chief, Cho said: "Well, Commanding General Ushijima, as the way may be dark, I, Cho, will lead the way."

Returning the bow, Ushijima replied: "Please do so, I will take along my fan since it is getting warm."

An hour later Ushijima and Cho stepped through a fissure in the cliff face overlooking the ocean.* It was about six feet high and six feet wide, opening upon a small ledge above the water. Both wore their dress uniforms, complete with medals and saber. A white quilt and a white sheet symbolizing death were laid over the ledge. Above them the moon had begun its descent.

They strolled out to the ledge, Ushijima calmly fanning himself. They bowed in reverence to the eastern sky, the customary obeisance to the emperor, and sat together on the white sheet and quilt. Only a hundred feet behind them were the approaching American soldiers. Having heard voices, they began hurling grenades, unaware that the Japanese generals were so close to them.

First Ushijima and then Cho bared their bellies to the upward thrust of the ceremonial knives in their hands. Upon the sight of blood the adjutant standing by with unsheathed saber delivered the coup de grâce.

Two shouts, two saber flashes—and it was done. And the moon began sinking into an obsidian sea.

---

* This account of Ushijima and Cho's final moments came from Ushijima's cook Tetsuo Nakamuta, who was a witness.

Epilogue:
The Value of Okinawa

Truth trying to overtake falsehood is like the sound of an explosion seeking to catch up with the flash, and this seems to be especially true of that greatest myth of World War II: the belief that the atomic bombs dropped on Hiroshima and Nagasaki in early August 1945 compelled Japan to surrender.

There is no question that these dreadful fireballs ushering in the Age of the Mushroom Cloud had much to do with Emperor Hirohito's decision to order his Imperial Conference to accept the Allied surrender offer. But before they were dropped—as has been suggested at the beginning of this narrative—Japan was already a defeated and demoralized nation, deeply divided between the diehards fiercely determined to continue the conflict regardless of the costs, and those timid members of the peace party who realized that the end had come but who still feared to risk the wrath of the firebrands. The atomic bombings, then, brought Hirohito to their side and encouraged them to defy the War Lords. But the fact remains that *before then*, before Okinawa, Japan was already beaten.

This was the conclusion of the most authoritative voice on

the subject, the U.S. Strategic Bombing Survey created by President Harry Truman to assess the effects of Allied bombing in World War II. It declared: "Based on a detailed investigation of surviving Japanese leaders involved, it is the Survey's opinion that certainly prior to 31st December, 1945, and in all probability prior to 1st November, 1945, Japan would have surrendered, even if the atomic bombs had not been dropped, even if Russia had not entered the war, even if no invasion had been planned or contemplated." No judgment could be more unequivocal. Why, then, were the bombs dropped?

Debate still rages over whether or not Japan should have been so ravaged. Harry Truman to his dying day insisted that he "never had any doubt" about the necessity of striking Nippon with atomic weapons. However, recent examination of his private papers produced a letter to his sister in which he wrote: "It was a terrible decision." Some critics claim that Japan was chosen rather than Germany because it was an Oriental nation—ignoring the fact that the Nazis had been destroyed in May, two months before the "Fat Boy" on its tower at Alamogordo flashed upward with a light not of this world—or that the thickening mood of savage revenge that had seized the American public had to be satisfied. Apart from such emotional conclusions, it should be obvious that the atomic bomb kept Stalin out of Western Europe and forced him to walk softly in Asia. This was indeed a strategic consideration of the highest order, one that no sincere statesman could refuse to balance against the hideous loss of life and property that would ensue under the mushroom cloud; together with the certainty that American declarations of desiring peace and prosperity for all peoples would henceforth have to be read in the light of those terrible fireballs. Nevertheless, the atomic bombs did indeed keep the Soviet Union out of Western Europe and curtailed its ambitions in the Far East, even though they also presented the Soviets with a powerful psychological stick with which to beat the United States and its Free World allies.

To these considerations must be added the convictions of many high-ranking naval and air commanders—none of them members of the Joint Chiefs of Staff—that Japan could be bombed, shelled, and blockaded into submission. This is probably true, but can never be proved. At best such a policy would indubitably have saved many American lives, even though it would almost certainly have caused horrible and unimaginable suffering in Japan. Because it would have taken so much longer, it would have given the insatiably land-hungry Stalin the opportunity to enter the war for a much longer period than his actual six-day contribution, and thus cloak him in the customary mane of the lion roaring for his "rightful" share of the spoils. Hiroshima, then, did save Japan from the brutal and selfish policies of her War Lords determined that the nation must die like a dutiful *Samurai*. But Nagasaki was absolutely unnecessary, coming only three days after Hiroshima and thus too close to influence any decision. Probably it was dropped to show Japan that the United States possessed more than one bomb—actually it had only two—and presumably could produce many more.

From all this speculation only two probabilities seem to emerge: one, that Japan was already beaten and would have surrendered before the monster Operation Olympic invasion began three months later; two, that Harry Truman dropped both bombs as much to frighten Stalin as to finish off Japan.

Where, then, does this leave Okinawa?

A corollary of the myth of the atomic bombs is the other though less widespread misconception of Okinawa as an unnecessary battle. Here is one more instance of that cart-before-the-horse thinking common to those facile minds so well described by Aristotle: "Contemplating little, they have no difficulty deciding." The Battle for Okinawa was begun on April 1, 1945, more than 4 months before the bombing of Hiroshima and 3½ months before the first bomb was exploded at Alamogordo. The Americans wanted Okinawa for a staging area only 375 miles from Kyu-shu, the Japanese hoped through its *kamikaze* corps either to cripple or destroy the enemy sea power that had brought the Americans so close to Japan proper.

Because Imperial General Headquarters had not the slightest suspicion that the Americans were close to producing an atomic bomb, General Ushijima and his Thirty-second Army expected to defend Okinawa with conventional weapons, while General Buckner intended to seize the Great Loo Choo with the same instruments of war. Not until just before Hiroshima were Fleet Admiral Nimitz and General of the Armies MacArthur—the of-ficers who would command the invasion of Japan—informed that their country now possessed atomic weapons. By then, of course, Okinawa had fallen—and when it did, it so shocked Emperor Hirohito that he could echo what Fleet Admiral Osami Nagano, his personal naval advisor, had cried when he learned of the loss of Saipan: "Hell is on us!"

Until Okinawa, Hirohito had been an accomplice of the War Lords; if not a willing one, then, in the words of MacArthur, who came to know him better than any other Westerner: "a figure-head, but not quite a stooge." After its fall, he was ready to chal-lenge them, and the atomic bombs gave him that opportunity.

So Okinawa was indeed decisive, for if the Japanese had won in this biggest battle of the Pacific War, the hold of the War Lords upon the nation of Nippon would have been so strength-ened that even the influence of Hirohito could not have per-suaded the Imperial Conference to accept the Allied surrender offer. Thus, the war would have been prolonged—hopelessly for Japan, of course—and only the production and use of more atomic bombs would have avoided that titanic clash of arms upon the Tokyo Plain.

Index